THE
FAST FACTS
ENCYCLOPEDIA

A N   L S
&   R E

© Aladdin Books Ltd 2000

Designed and produced by
Aladdin Books Ltd
28 Percy Street
London W1P 0LD

First published in the United States by
Copper Beech Books, an imprint of
The Millbrook Press
2 Old New Milford Road
Brookfield, Connecticut 06804

ISBN: 0-7413-0931-4

Printed in Italy

Some of the material in this book was previously
published in other Aladdin Books series.

THE
FAST FACTS
ENCYCLOPEDIA
OF

ANIMALS
& NATURE

Copper Beech Books
Brookfield, Connecticut

CONTENTS

INTRODUCTION

The Encyclopedia of Animals and Nature will amaze you with its range of fascinating topics. You will find out what dinosaurs ate, how birds fly, and everything you need to know about lions, butterflies and hurricanes! This encyclopedia has a clearly defined contents and a user-friendly index to help you find out all you can – everyone you know will be surprised and delighted by your knowledge of animals and nature!

Animals

The animal world is an enormous subject. There are thousands of different species within each animal group.

Learn all about all sorts of animals from lobsters to lions, and from birds to beetles!

Did you know what would happen if giraffes had short necks, or if elephants had no trunks? Find answers to questions you hadn't even thought of!

Read on and discover how wolves got their bad name, and what the difference is between crocodiles and alligators. Become an animal expert reading this book!

Nature

Do you know what tsunamis are and how they work? If not, read on and you will soon know all about these giant waves. Amaze your friends with your knowledge of the earth. Tell them what would happen if the earth stood still or if continents didn't move.

Find out how trees grow, what exactly weather is, and how snow, ice, and hail form.

You probably know that nature can do great damage sometimes. Read all about natural disasters like droughts and earthquakes. Find out how volcanoes erupt, and why floods happen.

When you next go to the beach, make sure you check this book to find out which creatures hide at the seashore!

This encyclopedia will take you on an exciting journey through the world of animals and nature. If you are interested in one particular topic, then look it up in the contents list to find out which pages cover it. With fantastic pictures and fun-to-read text, this Encyclopedia will give you lots of brilliant facts.

WHAT IF MAMMALS LAID EGGS?

You would need very strong eggshells! Fortunately, very few mammals actually lay eggs in the same way as birds and reptiles. Those that do, such as the bizarre-looking duck-billed platypus, are called *monotremes*. Other mammals give birth to live young. Some, called *marsupials*, carry the young in a pouch, while the rest keep the immature baby within a part of their body called the *womb*. Here it can grow and develop.

This period of time when the baby mammal is inside the mother is called the *gestation period*. Its length varies greatly, depending on the size of the animal. The human gestation period is about 270 days. The Asiatic elephant can carry its young for an astonishing 760 days. However, the Virginian opossum is pregnant for as little as eight days!

Egg-cellent parents!

There are only three species of mammal that actually lay eggs. These are the duck-billed platypus (above), the long-beaked echidna (right), and the short-beaked echidna, which all live in Australasia. The duck-billed platypus usually lays two eggs in an underground den. These eggs are covered in a tough leathery shell to protect them.

After about ten to twelve days in the den, the babies hatch from their eggs and feed on milk. This is produced by special glands on the mother.

Womb   Ovaries

Eggs without shells

Although most mammals don't lay eggs like
birds or reptiles, they all (including humans)
produce tiny, microscopic eggs from
organs inside the female, called *ovaries*.
After mating, these eggs may be
fertilized with sperm from the male,
they embed themselves into an area
of the mother's womb. The baby
grows here, protected from the
outside world and fed by
nutrients that pass from the
mother's blood. These nutrients
are passed from the mother to
the baby through an organ
called the *placenta*, and along
the umbilical cord. Once the
baby has developed enough, it
is born. It passes from the
womb, through the birth canal,
and out into the world.

Baby elephant

Birth canal

What if a kangaroo didn't have a pouch on its belly?

It would have to find some other way of carrying
around its young. Kangaroos give birth to very
immature, furless babies. The tiny creature has to
crawl through its mother's fur, into the pouch,
where it attaches itself to one of four milk teats.

The pouch is called a *marsupium*, and
mammals that have this are referred to as
marsupials. These include possums, opossums,
koalas, and wombats.

DRAGONFLY

*I*F YOU COULD GO BACK IN TIME, before the dinosaurs – 300 million years ago – then dragonflies would be the biggest flying creatures. They were the first large insects to appear on Earth. Some were the size of crows. They haven't changed much since, except to become smaller. Dragonflies are fierce hunters that catch small insects in midair.

ABDOMEN
Inside the long, thin abdomen are the usual insect innards of blood vessel along the top, guts in the middle, and main nerve along the bottom.

BREATHING TUBES

GUT

HEART

WINGS
The two pairs of see-through wings are held out sideways when resting.

EYES
Dragonflies have better eyes than all other insects. Each has more than 30,000 units, ommatidia, for incredible vision. A dragonfly can catch a tiny gnat in twilight (when we could barely see a tree).

FLYING MUSCLES

LEGS
In flight, the legs hang down to form a prey-catching "basket." Their sharp tips grip leaves or twigs when resting.

ANATOMY *AT WORK*
HOW FLIES FLY
The wings are joined to the rigid-cased thorax. This contains two sets of flight muscles. One set pulls the top of the thorax, which clicks down and flips the wings up (1). The other muscle set pulls the thorax in, making it thinner, so the top clicks back up again, flipping the wings down (2).

1

2

THE
F L Y
CLUB

NO IMPOSTERS

WHY AM I NOT A FLY?
Many insects called "flies" are not. True flies, like houseflies, bluebottles, crane flies, fruit flies, mosquitoes, gnats, and midges, have two wings. Pretend "flies," like dragonflies, damselflies, mayflies, stoneflies, and butterflies, have four wings.

BEETLE

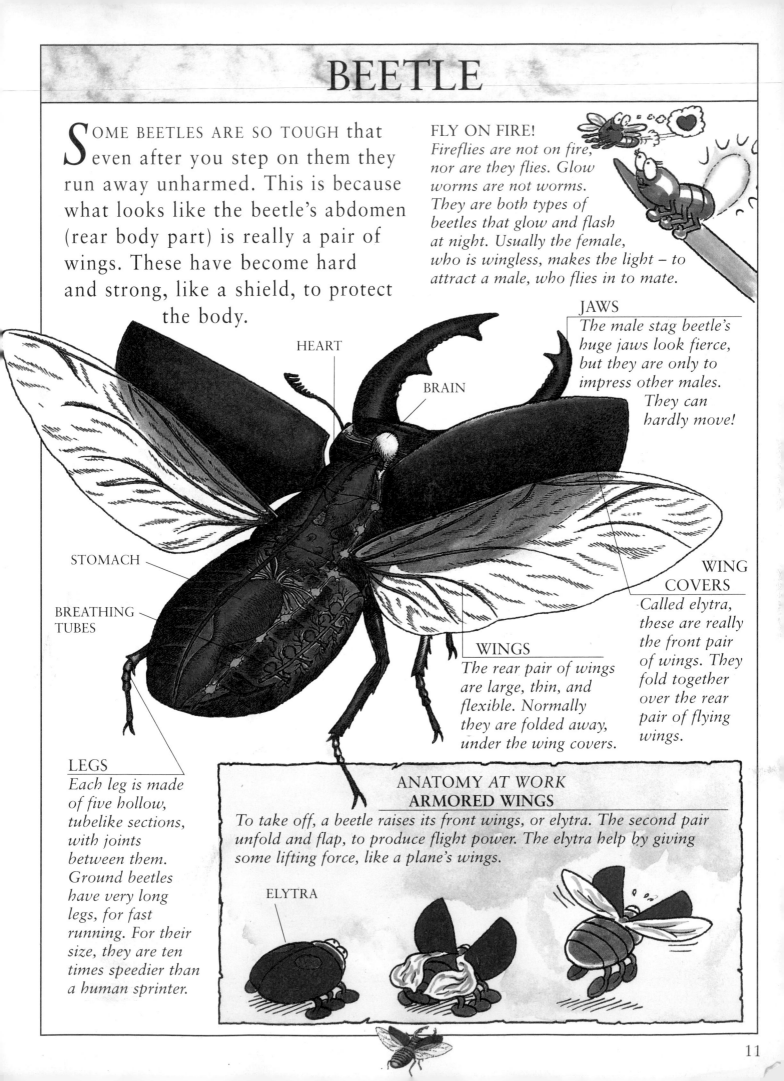

SOME BEETLES ARE SO TOUGH that even after you step on them they run away unharmed. This is because what looks like the beetle's abdomen (rear body part) is really a pair of wings. These have become hard and strong, like a shield, to protect the body.

FLY ON FIRE!
Fireflies are not on fire, nor are they flies. Glow worms are not worms. They are both types of beetles that glow and flash at night. Usually the female, who is wingless, makes the light – to attract a male, who flies in to mate.

HEART

BRAIN

JAWS
The male stag beetle's huge jaws look fierce, but they are only to impress other males. They can hardly move!

STOMACH

BREATHING TUBES

WING COVERS
Called elytra, these are really the front pair of wings. They fold together over the rear pair of flying wings.

WINGS
The rear pair of wings are large, thin, and flexible. Normally they are folded away, under the wing covers.

LEGS
Each leg is made of five hollow, tubelike sections, with joints between them. Ground beetles have very long legs, for fast running. For their size, they are ten times speedier than a human sprinter.

ANATOMY AT WORK
ARMORED WINGS

To take off, a beetle raises its front wings, or elytra. The second pair unfold and flap, to produce flight power. The elytra help by giving some lifting force, like a plane's wings.

ELYTRA

FISH OF SHORES & REEFS

The shallow waters along the seashore provide a wide range of fish habitats, from tidal mudflats to sandbanks and rocky coasts. In tropical areas, coral reefs can support a great variety of life. Nutrients are plentiful, and the bright sun provides lots of light, so many seaweeds and other plants can grow. These plants are the basic food for all the forms of animal life, including myriad worms, crabs, starfish and shellfish, which thrive in the warm, shallow waters. They, in turn, provide food for a dazzling array of fish. In contrast, the shoreline of a wide beach is much emptier of fish.

Nooks and crannies
The blenny and rock goby use rocks and boulders to shelter from predators and ambush prey. The clingfish can stick to overhanging rocks with its suckerlike fins.

Clingfish

Lumpsucker

Rock goby

Grunion

Butterfish

Blenny

Tropical paradise
Many people dream of "getting away from it all" on a deserted tropical island. In 1719 the English writer Daniel Defoe based his adventure story *Robinson Crusoe* on the experiences of a real sailor named Alexander Selkirk. The book tells of a lonely castaway struggling to survive on a small island, beset by lack of food, water and shelter, and plagued by insect pests, pirates and islanders. Not such a paradise?

Traditional fishing
Around the world's coastlines, people use various traditional fishing methods to catch what they need from the sea. The Inuit people of northern North America fish from the shore or along coastal rivers, using nets, and spears, harpoons and hooks carved from natural materials such as walrus tusks or whalebone. However, these traditional ways of life are becoming ever more difficult to preserve.

The perils of the tide

Shores and reefs can be treacherous places for fish, because of the tides. As the tide falls, it can leave fish marooned in pools. The butterfish is named from its tough, slippery, slimy skin. This enables it to wriggle from under rolling pebbles, and prevents it from drying out as it flaps over the rocks from one pool to another. Shore fish such as gobies and blennies can withstand great variations in temperature and salinity (salt concentration), as well as buffeting by waves and rolling boulders.

Partners in life

Certain fish team up with quite different animals, in relationships beneficial to both. Clownfish swim among the stinging tentacles of anemones. Their bodies are covered in mucus that provides a barrier to the stings. The clownfish are safe from attack while the anemone consumes the food they drop. This partnership is called symbiosis.

Porcupinefish

Blue-banded Angelfish

Clownfish

Butterflyfish

Regal tang

Coral Trout

Warm and shallow

Coral reefs are rich environments for fish and other sea life, but they form only in certain places around the world. The water must be very clean, and warm – preferably around 75°F all year – with a salt concentration of between 25 and 40 parts per thousand. The basis of the reef is the coral polyp, a tiny animal like a miniature jellyfish. Polyps grow in their millions and build hard, chalky cup-shaped skeletons around their bodies, for protection. As they die, more polyps grow on top. Over hundreds of years, billions of coral skeletons accumulate, and the rocky reef grows. The corals are food for hundreds of fish.

WHAT IF A BAT COULDN'T HEAR?

Clicks —
Echoes —

Bat sonar

The bat's sound pulses are so high-pitched that you or I couldn't hear them. However, a bat's hearing is so sensitive, it can hear these clicks and their echoes. The bat can find its way and catch its flying food even in complete darkness. The system is like radar, but with sound waves instead of radio waves. It's known as sonar or echolocation.

It would fly through the dark night – and crash into things! Mammals possess an amazing array of senses to detect the outside world. Hearing is only one of these. They are able to see in very poor light, smell the very faintest odors, taste an enormous variety of different foods, and detect touches and vibrations that are as light as a feather.

Dolphin sonar

Predatory members of the whale group, such as dolphins and killer whales, have a sonar system like the bat's (above). The sound pulses are concentrated, or focused, into a beam by a large lump in the forehead, the melon.

melon

What if whales could sing?

All whales make underwater sounds, varying from shrill clicks and squeaks and squawks, to haunting low moans and groans. Beluga and humpback whales are so noisy that their calls can be heard underwater more than 125 miles (200 km) away. The "songs" of a whale can last between 6 and 35 minutes, and are used by the whales to communicate with each other.

Nighttime eye-shine

If you've ever shone a flashlight into a cat's eyes, you will have seen that they appeared to glow in the dark. A cat's eye has a mirrorlike layer inside, the tapetum. Light rays come into the eye and some are detected by the light-sensitive layer, the retina. Others pass through the retina, bounce off the tapetum, and get sensed by the retina on the way out. This gives the eye two chances to detect light rays. Other nocturnal (nighttime) animals, such as opossums, have this too.

The pupil opens wider in dark conditions, to let in more light.

The retina detects light and turns it into nerve signals, which go to the brain.

The tapetum is a layer behind the retina. It reflects the light back onto the retina.

What if a lion had eyes on the side of its head?

It would leap at its prey, and probably miss! Most hunters, such as seals, cats, and foxes, have two forward-facing eyes at the front of the head. This gives them overlapping fields of vision (right), and allows them to judge distances well, for pursuit and pounce. Most hunted mammals, such as deer, zebras, and rabbits, have eyes on the sides of their head. Although this means that they can't judge distances well, it does give them a good overall view for spotting any predators that may be creeping up on them (right).

Something in the air

Dogs sniff everything, from the food they eat, to other dogs, especially when it is time to mate. The scent in the air enters the nose and attaches to an organ called the *olfactory bulb.* This is very large and very sensitive in a dog's nose. It then sends signals to the brain.

Olfactory bulb

NATURE'S BALANCE

The living world performs a delicate balancing act. Living things can only exist where conditions are right and they depend on each other for survival. Only a few living things can survive without oxygen from the earth's atmosphere. They all need water. They need the right climate and the right temperature, not too wet and not too dry, not too hot and not too cold. Above all, each living thing forms part of a system, depending on others for survival.

Biome

ECOSYSTEMS IN SCALE
Parrots in a rainforest and fish on a coral reef are part of different ecosystems. Taken together, creatures, plants and their habitat make up an ecosystem. The largest ecosystems into which the earth's land is divided are called biomes. For example, the tropical forest biome, which includes all tropical forests on every continent, takes up about one-fifth of all land. A community consists of the animals and plants in a small area. Within a community are populations, for example, all the rabbits in one wood.

Community

Two populations

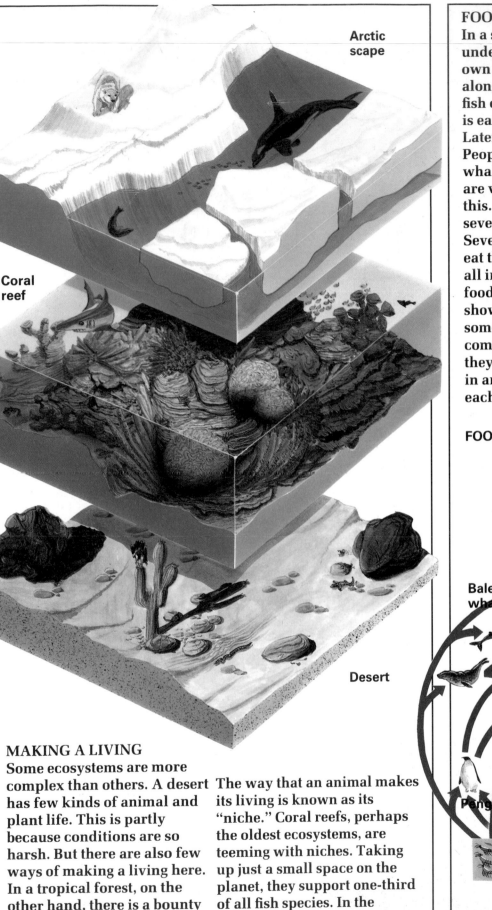

Arctic
scape

Coral
reef

Desert

MAKING A LIVING

Some ecosystems are more complex than others. A desert has few kinds of animal and plant life. This is partly because conditions are so harsh. But there are also few ways of making a living here. In a tropical forest, on the other hand, there is a bounty of trees, flowers, and other plants. Birds, monkeys, frogs, snakes and vast numbers of insects will all coexist.

The way that an animal makes its living is known as its "niche." Coral reefs, perhaps the oldest ecosystems, are teeming with niches. Taking up just a small space on the planet, they support one-third of all fish species. In the Arctic, where there are few niches, things look simpler. But even the simplest eco- system has a lot going on in it.

FOOD WEBS

In a simple food chain an underwater plant makes its own food. A shrimp comes along and eats the plant. A fish eats the shrimp, which is eaten in turn by a seal. Later, a whale eats the seal. People catch and eat the whale. In fact, food chains are very rarely as simple as this. Most animals eat several different foods. Several other animals may eat them. Food chains are all interwoven, forming a food web, like the one shown below. These can sometimes be very complicated indeed. But they show how living things in an ecosystem depend on each other for survival.

FOOD WEBS

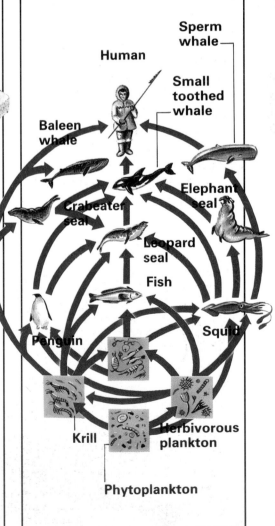

Sperm
whale

Human

Small
toothed
whale

Baleen
whale

Elephant
seal

Crabeater
seal

Leopard
seal

Fish

Squid

Penguin

Krill

Herbivorous
plankton

Phytoplankton

DOGS

The dog family, or Canidae, includes dogs, wolves, jackals, and foxes. Dogs tend to take advantage of any situation, feeding on carrion, insects, and even fruit and leaves, if they cannot hunt. They can all run at speed for long distances, but are less agile than cats. Dogs are intelligent, sociable animals and most live as tightly-knit family groups or packs, at least for part of the year. They communicate by sounds, body postures, and their highly developed sense of smell.

Domestic Dogs

The earliest remains of a domestic dog are believed to be over 11,000 years old. Abandoned wolf pups may have been taken into the home as pets, guard dogs, or hunters. Dogs treat the families they live with as members of their pack, taking their place in the hierarchy. As with other domestic animals, many different breeds have been produced, each with different characteristics.

Big Bad Wolf

Wolves have had a bad image for centuries because they kill domestic animals and game if they have to. There are many stories, but few proven cases, of attacks on people. Fairy stories about the Big Bad Wolf and legends of werewolves (right) reflect the fear of wolves. It has lead to centuries of persecution. Today the gray wolf, which once roamed most of the northern hemisphere, is an endangered animal. Efforts to re-introduce it involve improving its image.

Hot and Cold Foxes

The Arctic fox, as its name suggests, lives in the cold Arctic tundra. It can survive temperatures as low as -58°F. It has a coat of thick fur all over its body, even on the pads of its paws, and on its small, rounded ears. They are so well insulated that they lose very little heat.

Pavlov

Ivan Pavlov was a Russian doctor who spent a lot of time finding out how the human body works. He used dogs for his experiments. He discovered he could train them to salivate with a bell, not just in response to food. When the body learns to perform a function in response to an artificial cue it is called a conditioned reflex.

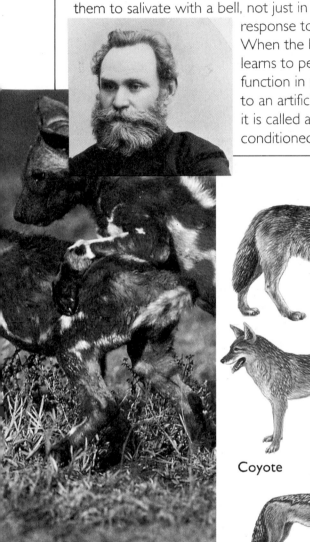

Peter and the Wolf

The Russian composer Prokofiev wrote this musical fairy tale for children in 1936. The story is told by a narrator and all the characters – Peter, his grandfather, the wolf, the bird, the cat, and the duck – are played by different musical instruments from the orchestra. The wolf is portrayed by three horns.

Wolf

Canine Relatives

The closest relatives of the domestic dog are wolves, coyotes, and jackals. Members of a wolf pack hunt together cooperatively to bring down large prey. The North American coyote is one of the few wild animals that is increasing in numbers today. An adaptable animal, it eats anything it can find. A breeding pair of African jackals stay mated for life.

Coyote

Jackal

Working Dogs

Many domestic dogs work for their living, helping on the farm or with field sports, racing and guarding or guiding their owners. Huskies, bred for their strength and resilience, work together in teams, pulling sleds across the snow.

The tiny Fennec fox, the smallest of all the wild dogs, lives in hot African deserts. It keeps itself cool by sleeping in a burrow during the hottest part of the day. It uses its huge ears as radiators to get rid of excess body heat. They are also useful for listening to the sounds of the tiny animals on which it feeds.

WHAT ARE FLOODS?

Floods are the waters which cover an area of land that is normally dry. They have affected almost every corner of the earth at some time or another, but those which cause the greatest amount of damage are the result of extreme weather conditions.

Tropical storms, which are called typhoons, hurricanes, or cyclones in different parts of the world, whip up the winds over the oceans and create huge waves. These waves, known as storm surges, race toward the shore and crash onto the coastline. The country of Bangladesh has suffered serious flooding on many occasions, as cyclones in the Bay of Bengal send huge sea waves crashing over the low-lying coastal areas. Other enormous waves which produce severe flooding are the so-called tidal waves, or *tsunamis*, which result from earthquakes or volcanic eruptions.

The millions of tons of rock, soil, and mud unleashed during a landslide can block a river valley or dam, causing water levels to rise dramatically. Flooding can also follow a seiche, the violent movement of lake waters following an earthquake. The most frequent cause, however, is when heavy rains and melting snow and ice make inland rivers and dams burst. This problem is made worse in areas where large numbers of trees have been cleared. Stripped of their vegetation, the hillsides cannot hold the excess water, which runs off and causes flooding in lowland areas.

◀ **During powerful storms, strong winds whip up high waves that pound down on the coastline. Sea defenses are often smashed to pieces, causing serious flooding in areas along the coast and extensive damage to property.**

► Sudden, violent bursts of water surging down narrow mountain valleys or dry river beds are called flash floods. These raging torrents of water, such as the one shown right at El Oued in Algeria, can flood an area for just a few hours, or even minutes, before subsiding.

Heavy rain falls during the summer monsoon season.

Volcanoes and earthquakes on the ocean bed cause *tsunamis*.

Swollen rivers burst their banks.

Storm surges cause flooding of lowland areas.

BIRDS

Birds, the champions of the air, are the most plentiful of the earth's warm-blooded animals. Scientists have estimated that there may be over 100,000 million birds in the world altogether. Their success is largely due to their ability to fly, which gives them versatility in finding food and places to live. Birds come in all different sizes and colors.

Brilliantly colored macaws live in noisy flocks in the world's rain forests. The species shown here are endangered in the wild.

Blue and yellow macaw

Scarlet macaw

The first birds
All living things change over thousands of years to improve their chances of survival. This process of change is called evolution. Birds evolved from reptiles about 150 million years ago. Their feathers developed from the scales which covered their ancestors. Wings gradually evolved from front legs. One of the first birds was **Archaeopteryx** *Archaeopteryx* ("ancient wing"). It was about the size of a gull and had the sharp teeth of a lizard. It was a poor flier and used to climb trees and then glide away.

Legend and symbol
Birds have been so successful that they can be found virtually everywhere. Over the years, different cultures have come into contact with birds and attached various meanings to them. Bird flight has always inspired awe in earthbound humans. Birds have often been viewed as bearers of good fortune. However, crows, vultures, and other carrion-scavenging birds are commonly associated with evil or horror.

The phoenix
This bird was worshiped in ancient Egypt, but exists only in legend. The phoenix was said to set itself on fire and then rise from its own ashes.

The dove
The dove as a symbol of peace originated with the biblical story of Noah, who sent a dove from his Ark to find dry land.

Bird skeleton

Skull

Wing bone — Vertebrae

Ribs

Wishbone
(Collarbone)

Tailbone

Breastbone

Pelvis — Leg bone

Inside a bird

Birds are vertebrates, with an internal skeleton and backbone. Flying birds have very light skeletons, to reduce the amount of weight they have to carry in flight. Many of their bones are hollow. The inside of the bone looks like a honeycomb. Birds also have lightweight beaks, instead of heavy, bony jaws.

Hyacinth
macaw

Scarlet
macaw

Bird records

There is an amazing variety of different bird species. Although all birds share similar body structure, they differ enormously in color, size, and shape. Some birds are so plentiful that they become pests. Others, like the California condor, are extremely rare.

Largest and smallest

The ostrich is the largest bird in the world. It can grow up to 9 feet (2.7m) tall. The smallest bird is the bee hummingbird of Cuba, which is no larger than a bumblebee.

Ostrich

Most common

The domestic fowl, also known as the chicken, is the world's most common bird. In the wild, the red-billed quelea of Africa is the most numerous bird.

Mute swan

Domestic fowl

The white stork

In Europe, the stork is a symbol of good luck. In legend, the stork delivers newborn babies to homes.

The pelican

The pelican got its reputation for being a dutiful parent in the Middle Ages (5-15th centuries). It was fabled to pierce its chest and feed its young with its blood.

Heaviest

The heaviest flying bird ever recorded was a mute swan that weighed 50 lb (23 kg). The Kori bustard can also grow to this weight.

RUNNING DINOSAURS

A lot of people imagine that dinosaurs plodded along at an extraordinarily slow pace. It is probably true that the giant plant-eating sauropods could only walk fairly slowly; if one of them had broken into a run, it would have fallen over or broken its bones. The medium-sized plant-eating ceratopsians however, may have trotted quite fast, just like modern rhinos. Some of the smaller meat-eaters could even have run as fast as a racehorse, especially *Ornithomimus* and the vicious *Deinonychus*. But how do paleontologists know how dinosaurs could run and swim when they all died out so long ago? And how can they work out how fast they could run?

Deinonychus

Modern animals use different ways of moving at different speeds. A horse can walk, trot, canter, and then gallop, as it moves faster and faster. Normally, the four legs move in pairs on opposite corners of the horse, but when galloping, both front legs and both hind legs move as pairs together. Some smaller dinosaurs may have been able to gallop, but most could only walk and trot, and the biggest could only walk.

Deinonychus was found in Wyoming, in the 1960s. It was only 10-13 feet long, but it had a huge toe claw that may have been used for slashing at plant-eaters.

Some of the best swimmers were the ichthyosaurs, which were not dinosaurs. These reptiles had powerful tails for swimming, and paddles for steering.

Ichthyosaurus

Evidence

When a dinosaur moved over damp mud or sand, it left footprints. These could then be covered with more sand which preserved the tracks. Fossil dinosaur footprints have been found all over the world. These can show which dinosaur made the track, where it was going, and how fast it was moving.

Migration

Recently, paleontologists have found some dinosaur footprint sites where there are thousands of separate trackways. In some cases, the tracks all head in the same direction, and appear to have been made by small and large animals of the same species. These trackways seem to be evidence that there were great herds of dinosaurs marching over long distances. Perhaps they were migrating in search of food or to find warmer winter climates.

These footprints show how the animals walked and how their legs were held. The mammal-like reptile (1) was a sprawler; a dinosaur ancestor (2) walked partly upright; the theropods (3) walked upright on two legs; and the ornithopod (4) could use all fours or walk upright.

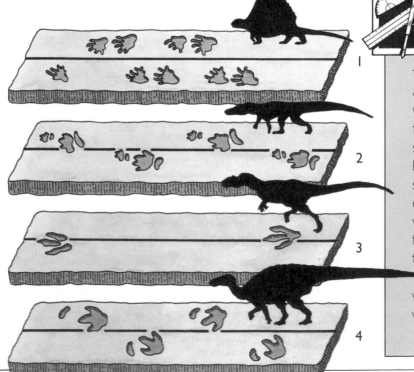

Calculating dinosaur speeds

The faster you run, the longer your strides become. You can test this by walking slowly, walking fast, and then running across some sand. Cover the same distance each time and figure out your various speeds by using a stopwatch. Now measure the distance between each footprint and plot your speed against your stride length. Scientists can calculate dinosaur speeds in the same way by looking at the spacing of their footprints. The wider apart the dinosaur tracks appear, the faster they must have been traveling. If the footprints are very close together, it's likely that they were walking along quite slowly.

POISONS AND STINGS

Animals use poisons for two reasons: to defend themselves against predators, and to overcome their own prey. Insects are no exception to this. Some have poisonous stings in their tails, some bite with poisonous jaws. Others are just poisonous all over. Insects that use poisons to catch prey are often masters of disguise. Those that use poisons for defense usually advertise the fact by having bright warning colors on their bodies, usually red- or yellow-and-black. Other insects are not poisonous, but mimic those that are.

Bee stings

Worker honeybees will defend the hive quite literally with their lives. The sting at the end of the worker bee's abdomen is a sac full of poison connected by a tube to a sharp, barbed spine. When the bee stings, the barbs make sure the sting stays in the victim while the venom is pumped into the wound. But they also mean that when the bee flies off, the end of its abdomen is torn away and it then dies.

Plates pump venom.

Bulb full of venom

Venom sac

Worker bee

Sting remedies

Bees and wasps only sting when they feel threatened, so you are more likely to get stung if you shout or wave your arms to drive one away. If you are stung by a bee, remove the sting with tweezers, taking care not to squeeze the poison sac. Wasps will not leave their sting in your skin if you allow them to remove it.

Wash the wound thoroughly with antiseptic, and put a cold, damp cloth on it to relieve the pain. Bee and wasp stings are not dangerous unless the swelling blocks the throat, or unless the victim who has been stung has an allergy to insect stings.

Lethal weapon

The bodies of some kinds of insects are poisonous, and taste disgusting. This provides a good defense against predators who recognize the species, and do not attack it. Some squirt stinging liquids, others have irritating hairs that get stuck in an attacker's skin. The grubs of a South African leaf beetle are so poisonous that Kalahari bushmen (right) use them to tip the ends of their arrows.

Ragwort is a poisonous weed common in European fields. But the caterpillars of the cinnabar moth are able to feed on the plant, and store the poisons in their body tissues. A bird who eats one will become very sick. These caterpillars have yellow-and-black warning stripes on their bodies to advertise their identity. Birds learn after only one experience to leave them alone.

Insects in folklore medicine

The bodies of blister beetles contain an irritating fluid called cantharidin which these insects use to defend themselves against predators. Before modern medicines were developed, doctors used to apply this substance to their patients' skin as a treatment for warts. The blisters caused by the fluid were also thought to allow the escape of poisons that built up inside the body. Bee stings were thought to cure rheumatism, so bees were allowed to sting the inflamed joints of rheumatic patients.

Proverbial insects

Traditional sayings or proverbs often refer to the familiar characteristics of common insects to help describe people's behavior. A group of people working very hard at a joint task are sometimes called "busy bees." If someone has a particular concern which others may not share, they are said to have a "bee in their bonnet." Children who will not sit still and concentrate at school are said to have "ants in their pants." Can you describe someone who has a "butterfly mind?"

Bee in your bonnet

Beetle chemists

Bombardier beetles use a spectacular chemical reaction as a powerful weapon against attackers. The beetle has special chambers in its abdomen where it stores two chemicals, each fairly harmless on its own. When the beetle is alarmed it mixes the chemicals in another chamber, together with an enzyme, which aids the reaction. A rocket-like jet of hot, poisonous spray shoots from the end of the abdomen. The beetle can direct the spray by twisting its abdomen towards a victim. The boiling chemicals produced cause painful blisters.

CUDDLY KILLERS

In the still of the early morning, a group of Inuit hunters in northern Canada heard a scuffling noise outside their tent. Suspecting a thief, one of the men went to investigate. It was indeed a thief – not a human one, but a massive polar bear! Terrified, the hunter edged toward the tent.

The great white beast followed, rearing up on its hind legs (*main picture*). Seconds later, a blow from the bear's powerful paw snapped his neck. Polar bears, the world's largest carnivores, are said to be the only bears that deliberately hunt humans for food. One explanation is that the weak-eyed creatures mistake Inuits dressed in sealskin clothing for their favorite food – seals!

Grizzly Swipes
The grizzly bear (Ursus horribilis, below right) *is an aggressive cousin of the brown bear. It does not hug its enemies to death, as once believed, but swipes at them with deadly 6-inch claws. Despite being 7 feet tall and weighing 1,100 pounds, it can run faster than an Olympic sprinter!*

UN–BEAR–ABLE?
The intelligent brown bear (*above*) was once common in many parts of Europe. It is now found in north and central Asia and North America. In colder habitats the beasts hibernate during the winter.

Bears generally prefer to avoid people. Although vicious if threatened (especially if guarding cubs), the brown bear is not normally dangerous. But stay clear of the Asian black bear – although small, it is unpredictably vicious!

Brown Bear

Black Bear

Big Drifters
Polar bears, distinguished by their white fur, long necks, and small heads, inhabit the Arctic Ice Cap, Greenland, Canada, and Russia.

Drifting on ice floes, they have traveled as far south as Iceland. Thick fur (which covers the pads of the feet to help grip the ice) and layers of fat enable them to survive the freezing conditions. They supplement their usual diet of fish and seals (and the occasional person!) with berries and grass.

FURRY ANCESTORS

Humans have always thought that bears were very special creatures. This has not always been to their advantage – prehistoric peoples sacrificed them to the gods. Celtic goddesses, such as Artio (*left*), were also shown as bears, while early Christians thought they carried the devil (*right*)! Some primitive peoples believed humans were descended from a bear, the "Animal Master."

Hey, Good Licking!

The saying "licked into shape" comes from the belief that this is what mother bears did to their cubs, who were born without shape! "Teddy" bears are named after big game-hunting president Theodore Roosevelt, who in 1902 refused to shoot a bear cub.

STARRY BEARS

In Greek myth, bears were sacred to Artemis, goddess of hunting. When the nymph Callisto had a son by the god Zeus, his jealous wife changed her into a bear. The nymph and her son eventually became stars – the Great (*above*) and Little Bear constellations are still named after them.

THOR'S BEARS. In Northern Europe the bear, rather than the lion, was the King of Animals. The Viking god Thor (*right*) kept two bears: Alta (the mother of all things female) and Alti (the father of all things male).

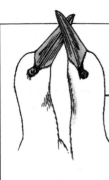

BIRD COURTSHIP

Birds need to find a suitable partner to mate with and breed. The male birds usually do the chasing, and competition among them is fierce. They have various ways of wooing females. Some show off their nest building or hunting skills, or give displays of dancing and singing. Some adopt more colorful feathers just for the breeding season. Puffins grow even more colorful beaks, which molt when the season is over.

Impressive pouch
Male frigate birds have bright red pouches of skin on their throats. To attract a female, they inflate these like giant balloons, sometimes for several hours. When a female bird chooses her mate, she rubs her head against his pouch.

Frigate bird

Ruff

Attractive feathers
Male ruffs perform their courtship display on communal grounds, called leks. Males defend a small patch, where they can show their feathers.

Good provider
Some male birds, like this British robin, bring the female a gift of food. This shows her whether the male is going to be a good provider of food.

Robin

Survival of the fittest
Male birds of different species have a wide variety of ways to attract a mate. These range from the beautiful plumage of a peacock to the elegant dance of a riflebird. The reason for courtship displays is that the males need to impress prospective mates. If a male's appearance or display is effective in attracting females, he will be able to pass on the characteristics which made him successful. In this way, traits that help an animal reproduce gradually spread to the whole species. This is one aspect of evolution.

Charles Darwin was the British naturalist who developed the theory of evolution in the 1850s.

The female riflebird (left) is wooed each year by the male's amazing dance.

Blue bird of
paradise
displaying his
tail fan

Amazing display

Among the most spectacular of all animals are
some male birds of paradise, such as this blue
bird of paradise. They grow long, brilliantly
colored feathers and plumes just for the
breeding season. To win over a female, they
perch on a branch, then swing upside down
and fan out their magnificent feathers. Several
birds may display on the same tree. The female
then faces the task of choosing the most
beautiful to mate with. The male molts his
display plumes at the end of the season, and
grows them again the following year.

Attracting attention

For hundreds of years, native peoples of
New Guinea have decorated themselves in
the courtship display feathers of birds of paradise to
make themselves more attractive. Elaborate feather
headdresses are worn in tribal dances to impress
members of the opposite sex. Although many birds
were killed for this tradition, birds of paradise were
not under serious threat until 1522, when Eiropeans
caught their first glimpse of one brought back on a
Spanish trading ship. By the end of the nineteenth
century, bird of paradise feathers were in such
demand for European fashion that the birds began to
decline seriously. They are now protected and most
species are slowly recovering their numbers.

New
Guinea
tribesman

BEETLES

In terms of numbers, the group of beetles, or Coleoptera, has been more successful than any other kind of animal. There are at least 370,000 known species in the world, and new ones are being discovered all the time. Beetles are armor-plated insects. The head and thorax are covered in tough cuticle, formed into strange, threatening shapes in many species. Despite their heavy appearance, most beetles fly very well. Beetle grubs undergo complete metamorphosis to become adult.

Some species of beetles are herbivores (plant-eaters), others are carnivores (meat-eaters). Some kill prey and eat it. Many perform the important function of consuming the dead bodies of animals, some eating the flesh, others eating fur or feathers. Some feed on animal dung. Some beetle pests consume grains or vegetables. Colorado beetles attack potato crops. Others attack vegetation, such as elm bark beetles that spread Dutch elm disease.

Weevil

Burying beetle

Most beetles have biting jaws to seize their prey. In weevils the jaws are located on the end of a long nose or rostrum.

Light show
Glowworms, or fireflies, are neither worms nor flies. They are beetles that produce light to attract mates. During dark evenings, males and females flash signals to each other, like morse code signals from a lantern. The code is different for each species. In South-East Asia, whole trees pulse with thousands of these tiny lights. The light is made by a chemical reaction involving an enzyme which releases energy in the form of light.

Holy beetle

The female scarab beetle rolls a ball of dung to her burrow. She lays her eggs in the dung, and the larvae feed on it. The scarab beetle was sacred to the ancient Egyptians. They compared the insect's behavior with the action of their god Ra, who, they believed, rolled the sun across the sky each day. Egyptian craftsmen made scarab jewelry, using gold, lapis lazuli, and semi-precious stones.

Rove beetle

Chafer beetle

Many kinds of beetles have fierce-looking jaws and horns. These are often for show, to frighten off predators, or for fighting between males. Stag beetles (left) are so named because the male has fearsome, antlerlike jaws. Sparring stag beetles wrestle, each trying to turn his opponent over. In beetles, the front pair of wings form tough, often colorful wing cases, called elytra. These fold back when the insect is not flying, to protect the delicate wings beneath. In flight, the wing cases are raised.

Elytron

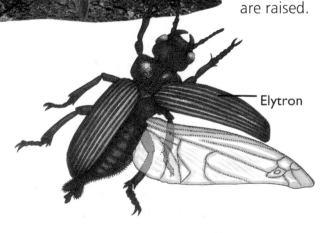

Insect machines

Some engineers have used insects as inspiration in the design and manufacture of machines. In the late 1940's the vehicle manufacturer Volkswagen pioneered a family car with a rounded beetle shape. Its success was phenomenal, and over 19 million Volkswagen Beetles were produced and exported to nearly 150 countries worldwide.

Heralds of death

Deathwatch beetles are wood borers. The larvae live in the dead wood of trees or in cut timber such as the roof timbers of a house. At mating time the males and females call to each other from the tunnels they have bored, tapping their jaws on the wood, and making an ominous ticking noise. In the days before pest control and when illnesses were difficult to treat, this sound in old houses was thought to foretell a death in the family, ticking away the last minutes of someone's life.

WATER POLLUTION

Humans use enormous quantities of water. Not only do we drink it, we use it to wash and bathe. We irrigate farm crops and gardens. We use it to flush away waste in the sewage system. Flowing water provided the first source of energy to power machines. Today's factories still use water to make things, or sometimes just to cool machinery. Hydroelectric power is an important source of energy in some countries. Our need for water makes it hard to find enough. We dam valleys to trap water in reservoirs – but this may disturb a river's flow. We sink boreholes – but these may dry out the land and stop springs flowing. Many human activities leave water dirty, and sometimes full of unwanted and dangerous chemicals. How to stop this pollution is one of the biggest problems we now face.

POLLUTING WATER
Detergents and poisonous chemicals are an obvious danger to water. But even chemicals that make things thrive, such as fertilizers, can create problems. If they run off the land into water they can make tiny water plants grow too well. These may use up all the oxygen in the water.

Sewage plant discharges into river.

Boreholes reduce the underground water level.

Factories discharge waste into rivers.

SEWAGE TREATMENT

Water and solids flow into the sewage treatment plant (1). This is filtered to remove solids and germs (2). Solid sludge may be stored to rot (3), or dried and used as fertilizer or burned (4). The remaining liquid is cleaned and returned to a nearby river (5).

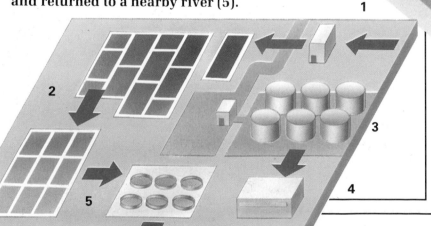

Oil tankers and refineries leak oil into the sea.

Rain can be acid.

Vegetation affected

Acid snow

Acid rain forms.

Solids deposited

Pollution

Wind

**Dams
disrupt
a river's flow.**

Factories

**Fertilizers, pesticides and
animal wastes spread on land
may be washed into water.**

ACID RAIN

Power plants produce
sulfur dioxide and nitrogen
oxides when they burn coal.
If these are not filtered out,
they are pumped into the air
from huge chimneys.
Carried by wind, polluted
clouds can make rain very
acidic hundreds of miles
away. This rain can kill
trees, damage other plants,
and make water too acidic
for fish. Acid snow can also
damage countryside.

DANGER IN THE FOOD CHAIN

Some substances that are used
to control pests break down
soon after they are used. But
some do not, and these may be
passed up the food chain to
animals which are not the
original target of the poison.
The poison can build up to
harmful levels in animals at
the top of the chain.

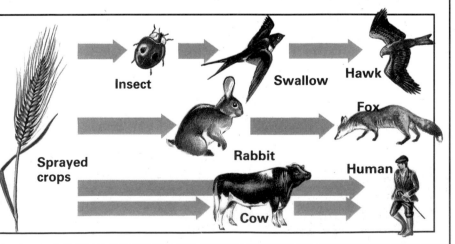

Insect

Swallow

Hawk

Fox

Rabbit

Human

Sprayed
crops

Cow

WHEN A VOLCANO ERUPTS

Volcanoes are in a sense the safety valves in the earth's crust, releasing the buildup of pressure caused by gases beneath the earth's surface.

The strength of a volcanic eruption depends on the type of magma and the amount of gases trapped in it. The magma formed when plates pull apart is very fluid. The gases in it have time to escape and there is no violent eruption. When plates collide, however, the magma formed is much thicker and stickier. Gases become trapped in it and escape explosively in a huge cloud of steam and dust thousands of feet high.

Surges of red-hot lava flood out of the volcano's crater at speeds of up to 600 ft per second. Lava will flow from the volcano as long as there is enough pressure to force it to the surface. After such violent eruptions, the entire volcano often collapses into its empty magma chamber, forming a steep-sided depression. This is called a caldera.

A volcano may be quiet for many years before it erupts again. Often its slopes are covered with grass and trees, like an ordinary mountain. A thin wisp of vapor rising from the crater may be the only sign that it is a still-active volcano.

The explosion
When a volcano erupts, the gases dissolved in the magma are released. If the vent is blocked by a plug of hardened lava, the trapped gases escape with a deafening explosion.

The buildup
There are often signs that a volcano is going to erupt. The ground starts to shake. The sides of the cone bulge out as magma collects inside it. There is a smell of sulfur as gases escape through cracks in the rocks.

▲ A fountain of molten lava erupts from a fissure on Hawaii's Kilauea volcano in 1983. Molten lava can reach temperatures of over 1,800°F.

▼ A plastic skin often forms over fast-flowing, runny lava. The skin is dragged into picturesque folds by the still-liquid lava running beneath it.

Afterwards

As well as lava and ash, the volcano belches out clouds of steam which condense into water. If there is a lot of steam, it falls as rain and mixes with the ash to form a thick mud. This may pour downhill, burying towns and villages.

The Gila Monster of the North American deserts is a lizard with a venomous bite. Its venom is powerful enough to subdue its bird and mammal prey.

The Australian Stump-tailed Skink is able to store food in its tail, as fat, and can go for months without food.

Gila Monster

Stump-tailed Skink

Desert Lizards

The Lizard group is by far the largest group of reptiles living today. Lizards can be found in many different environments. Many species of lizards live in the deserts. Lizards are well adapted to living in dry habitats. Their bodies are geared to retain water; they have very dry and scaly skin which loses water at a very slow rate.

Lizards also burn fat very slowly, therefore they are able to go for long periods of time without food. This is useful in dry desert areas where food is quite scarce.

A Frilled Lizard runs on its back legs to keep its body away from the hot sand. ▷

HAIR & FUR

Mammals keep themselves warm with fur or hairs which trap a layer of insulating air. Most have two kinds of fur – a thick layer of soft under-fur, and a thin layer of long guard hairs. Hair is coated with a waterproof substance called sebum which helps keep the animal dry. Hair comes in different colors and patterns which are used for recognition or camouflage, and it must be kept clean. Many mammals use grooming to cement social relationships; hair is sensitive to touch.

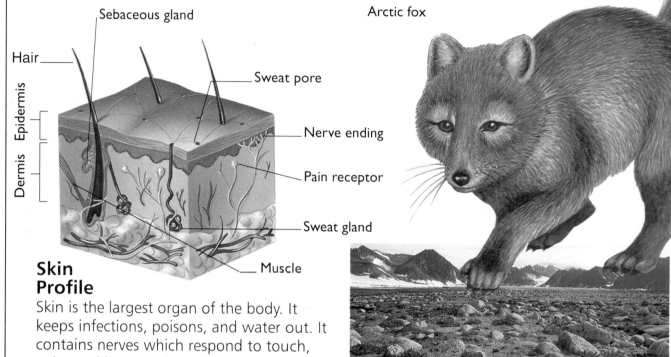

Sebaceous gland

Hair

Epidermis

Dermis

Sweat pore

Nerve ending

Pain receptor

Sweat gland

Muscle

Arctic fox

Skin Profile

Skin is the largest organ of the body. It keeps infections, poisons, and water out. It contains nerves which respond to touch, pain, and heat, and can repair itself when it gets damaged. It is the main temperature-regulating organ. Each hair grows from a tiny hole or follicle, which has a nerve, a muscle, blood vessels, and a sebaceous gland.

Prickles and Scales

Hair is made from a hard substance called keratin. Some mammals have sharp, rigid hairs in their coats. These spines form an excellent protection from predators. Hedgehogs roll up into a prickly ball when threatened, while porcupines turn their backs on their enemy and run — backward! Pangolin hair is modified to form scales. But the armor plating of armadillos is made from bony plates in the skin. When pangolins or armadillos roll themselves up they are safe from attack.

Armadillo

Fierce Warriors

In Papua New Guinea the native people often argue over territory. Their battles are usually ceremonial, but they dress up in huge headdresses (made from fur and feathers), and pierce their skin with echidna spines to look fierce.

The Arctic fox changes its coat from snowy white in winter to rocky brown in summer, making it difficult for predators to see. It also helps it creep up on *its* prey, the Arctic hare.

Spots and Stripes

As Rudyard Kipling says in the *Just So Stories*, giraffe blotches, zebra stripes, and leopard spots are a good disguise when the animals are in the dappled light under trees. But how do zebra stripes work out in the open? Some scientists think they might be an optical illusion which confuses or dazzles predators, making it difficult for them to launch a chase. Others think the stripes help zebras recognize members of their own herd, so they can keep together.

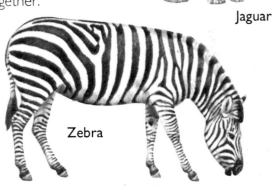

Jaguar

Zebra

Let your hair down!

Rapunzel was a beautiful young girl who had been locked in a tower by a wicked witch. During her captive years the girl's hair had grown to an extraordinary length. Every day the witch climbed up the thick plait of hair with food. Then a handsome prince came by and used the same trick to rescue Rapunzel. They lived happily ever after, but could this story be true? Human hair is stronger than steel fibers and the record for the longest hair is 13 feet, 6 inches. But hair this length is usually very brittle.

Fashionable Furs

In the last century, wearing the furry skins, or pelts, of beautiful mammals became fashionable. Hunting and trapping became big business. Millions of minks, foxes, seals, sea otters, and sables were killed and many, as a result, are close to extinction. Today many people object to killing animals for the sake of fashion (left), and campaign against the fur trade.

WHALES AND PORPOISES

There are 2 major types:
Toothed whales (66 species), including river dolphins, beaked whales, dolphins and porpoises.
Whalebone (baleen) whales (10 species), including gray whale, rorquals and right whales.
Biggest species: Blue whale – more than 100 ft (30 m) long and weighing 140 tons.

The whale family comprises mammals completely adapted to life in water. The majority of the 80 or so species live in the open seas, and of these, many inhabit warm tropical waters, while others spend much of their lives in the cool polar seas. All are mammals that during evolution returned to the sea, where animal life began. They still have a fish-like appearance. Among them are the biggest animals ever to have lived on Earth, with the Blue whale at 140 tons. Whales have no hind limbs or external ears. Their forelimbs take the form of paddles, and they have a tail with flukes. Beneath the skin is a layer of blubber, or fat, which helps to conserve body heat in the water.

Breathing

Whales can stay under water for an hour or more. Yet they breathe air with their lungs and must surface to replace the oxygen their bodies need. They store oxygen in their muscles and on a dive use this and the oxygen in their lungs to stay alive. As they surface, they open the blowhole on top of their head and blow out the used air. Then they take one or more deep breaths. Underwater, the blowhole is closed by a valve and the windpipe is sealed off from the throat to prevent water entering the lungs when the animal feeds.

Birth

Most whales do not reach maturity for many years. Pregnancy lasts from 8 months, for small dolphins, to 16 months or more for the big whales such as the blue, fin and sperm whales. Mostly only one offspring is produced. The baby is born under water tail-first. Immediately it surfaces, or its mother nudges its head out of the water, to take its first breath. The baby suckles milk from nipples hidden in folds on the mother's underside. Care of the young lasts weeks or months and is often carried out by all the females in a group.

A fin whale blows water out of its blowhole.

A mother dolphin and her offspring

Feeding

Whales are divided into two main groups by the different types of jaws and feeding methods.

Toothed whales have narrow lower jaws and, as adults, cone-shaped pointed teeth in the lower or both jaws. The teeth number from 2 to 120 depending on the species. In nar-whals, one of the two upper-jaw teeth is greatly enlarged to form a spirally twisted tusk 2m (6.5ft) in length. Toothed whales feed mainly on fish and squid.

Baleen, or whalebone, whales lack teeth and the upper jaw is V-shaped and has up to 300 plates of horny material similar to matted hair or fingernails. These plates of baleen hang down from the jaw and act as strainers to sift out plankton, the tiny aquatic animals and plants. When baleen whales are not feeding, the plates are enclosed within the broad lower jaw.

A southern right whale feeding on plankton

A killer whale hunts in the Arctic Ocean.

Migration

There tend to be many separate populations of whales. Some inhabit just the Northern Hemisphere, others the Southern, and within each there are Pacific, Atlantic and Indian Ocean groups. Within each area, groups of whales may migrate many thousands of miles each year, following definite circuits. These sometimes take them close to the mainland or among the pack ice of polar regions. Most toothed whales migrate to keep up with the movements of the fish on which they feed. Among baleen whales, the males move north in summer and return to the tropics in winter for the breeding season.

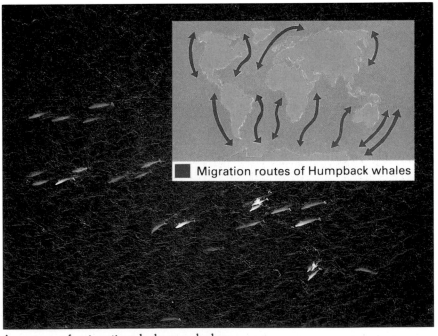

Migration routes of Humpback whales

A group of migrating beluga whales

FLIGHT OF BIRDS

The champions of the air, birds can fly faster and farther than any other animals. This has given them a great advantage over other creatures, allowing them to exploit food sources far and wide and escape from danger. Birds fly in different ways. Albatrosses soar and glide on rising currents of air. Hummingbirds hover in front of flowers by beating their wings an incredible 90 times a second. Other birds flap their wings with powerful strokes.

Male Anna's hummingbird hovering

Laysan albatross braking in flight

Flapping flight
In this most common method of flight, huge muscles in the bird's breast contract to push the wing down. Then tendons act as pulleys and pull the wing back up.

Famous flight
The Ancient Greek legend of Icarus has been the subject of many paintings and poems. Icarus was the son of a brilliant inventor named Daedalus. Both were imprisoned on the island of Crete. Daedalus crafted two pairs of wings so they could escape. The wings worked well and Daedalus flew to freedom. However, Icarus enjoyed flying so much that he flew too close to the sun. The wax which attached his wings melted and Icarus plunged into the sea and drowned.

Icarus

Flightless birds
There are 10 families of flightless birds. Scientists believe that some flightless species, such as ostriches and emus, evolved from birds that were never able to fly because they were too heavy. But most of today's flightless birds are thought to have gradually lost the ability to fly because flight was not necessary to their survival. These species are mainly found on islands in the Southern Hemisphere where they have few natural predators. Unfortunately, when many flightless birds came into contact with humans they had no defense or means of escape. The giant moa of New Zealand was an enormous flightless bird that grew up to 13 ft (4 m) tall. It was hunted to extinction by humans some 600 years ago.

Giant moa

AIRFOIL SHAPE

Wing

Air

Falcon wing

A bird's whole body is designed for flight. Its wings are shaped like airfoils, flat underneath and slightly curved from front to back on top. As the bird flies, air flows over its wing. As it does so, the airfoil shape creates an area of high pressure under the wing and an area of low pressure above it. This pushes the wing, and the bird, upward. This design is so successful that it is also used for aircraft wings.

Flip book flight

Animation is a sequence of pictures that, when passed quickly before the eyes, looks like it is moving. You can animate the flight pattern of a bird: swooping, flapping, bouncing, or wheeling. Make a small notebook with blank pages. Choose a bird to illustrate and draw it in flight. On each page, draw the bird in its next stage of flying, like the examples below. When you have drawn each page, flip through the book quickly. The bird will look like it is flying.

Eagle

Chaffinch

Mallard

Flightless cormorant
There are many species of cormorants that can fly, but the flightless species lives only on the Galapagos Islands off the coast of Ecuador. Its small wings are useful when it dives for fish.

Kiwi
The kiwi of New Zealand is active only at night. It has no visible wings or tail. To get from place to place, it breaks into a waddling run.

Penguins
Penguins slowly adapted from fliers to expert swimmers. This is because the icy lands of the Southern Hemisphere where they live are barren of life, but the ocean is full of food. Their wings act as flippers which help them to "fly" underwater.

Emu
The emu is an Australian bird that can grow to nearly 17 feet (2 m). Like an ostrich, it has long, strong legs and feet which enable it to run at great speeds. Emus generally run at slower speeds so that they can travel long distances without tiring.

CLIMATE CHANGE

Weather changes from day to day, season to season, and even over longer periods of time. The climate of a region may change altogether. For example, the Sahara used to be a grassland thousands of years ago. Now it's a desert. Because of the pollution we continually pump into the atmosphere, we could be drastically changing the atmosphere ourselves. Recent winters in the Alps have seen many places without their usual cover of snow. This could be a sign of climatic change.

THE GREENHOUSE EFFECT
The amount of carbon dioxide in the atmosphere has increased slightly in the last 100 years. It is believed this increase is caused by the burning of fossil fuels and destruction of rainforests. If the buildup continues, more heat will be trapped in the atmosphere and an increase in the average temperature over the earth may occur (global warming).

ICE AGES

There have been several Ice Ages when the climate of the earth was colder than average. Ice that spread from the poles and glaciers covered much of Europe and North America. The last Ice Age ended 10,000 years ago. Some scientists think that the world is returning to an Ice Age climate. But more people fear global warming.

Some heat escapes.

Cities and factories produce waste gases.

Heat is reflected back toward the earth.

WEATHER WATCH

You can keep tabs on the weather in your area. You can make a rain gauge and measure how much falls each day. You can record wind direction, either with a weather vane or a wind sock. You may be able to estimate wind speeds, too. How damp is the atmosphere? You can get complicated instruments to measure this, or you could just use an old pinecone, and notice whether it is open (dry) or closed (damp). Measure the temperature, too. Put a thermometer outside, but in the shade. You could make a chart of temperature and rainfall for each month. You would need to keep up your record for a long time, though, before you could even begin to guess whether the climate was changing!

Heat radiation from the sun

CFCs

CFCs are chemicals used in aerosol cans, refrigerators and in making styrofoam. If released into the air, they break down when exposed to ultraviolet light, giving off chlorine. The danger is that this chlorine may attack the ozone that forms a protective layer from ultraviolet radiation in the atmosphere. Already, environmentalists have detected ozone damage.

Homemade rain gauge made from a plastic bottle that has the top cut off and sitting upside down in the base.

Make a card for each month and measure temperature, rainfall and record other observations such as animals seen or trees.

Take average rainfall and temperature and make graphs for each. Use symbols for such things as falling leaves.

Rainforest destruction

FEBRUARY

DATE	TEMP.	RAIN	OBSERVATIONS
1	46°F	0	FRESH, CLEAR DAY
2	48°F	0	CLOUDY DAY
3	46°F	1mm	BLUSTERY, RAINY
4	44°F	0	COLD, CLEAR DAY. BULBS
5			
6			
7			
8			
9			
10			
11			
12			
13			
14			
15			
16			
17			
18			
19			
20			
21			
22			
23			
24			
25			
26			
27			
28			

RAIN

JAN FEB MAR APR MAY JUN JUL AUG SEP OCT NOV DEC

HOW INSECTS FEED

Insects have adapted to make use of every possible food source. Some feed on plants and some on animals. Some suck juices, while some munch on solid food. Many insects consume their prey while it is still alive; many more eat it when it is dead. Some insects are specialized to eat wood or pollen, feathers or blood, even dung. Some eat each other. Many insects feed on humans, causing illness by infecting people with tiny disease organisms. Insects that eat our food can cause famine. Those that eat building materials can cause great damage.

Insect species have different kinds of mouthparts, specialized to cope with their particular diet. All have four main structures. The mandibles are hard jaws for biting, the maxillae are secondary jaws. The labrum and the labium form the upper and lower lips. Caterpillars of butterflies and moths have strong jaws to munch leaves.

Ant

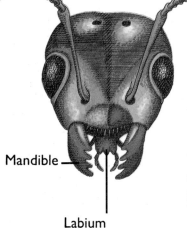

Mandible —

Labium

Biting
Ants' saw-shaped mandibles are closed by strong muscles to chomp on solid food. Behind the mandibles, the maxillae taste the food. The labium and labrum chew it and push it into the mouth.

A monarch butterfly caterpillar consumes a leaf.

Food chains
Insects form very important links in food chains, eating plants and in turn being eaten by other insects and larger animals. In temperate climates such as Europe, when the weather warms in spring and the buds on trees begin to burst, thousands of insect eggs hatch into grubs which begin to feed and grow. They provide food for the young of nesting birds such as blackbirds and robins. Swallows return from their warm wintering grounds in South Africa just as the grubs are turning into adult insects. This provides an airborne feast for the swallows (right) to feed to their young as they hatch.

Butterfly

Proboscis

Locust pests
In Africa, the feeding habits of migratory locusts make them one of the most feared of pests. These insects are usually solitary, and dull in color. But when rains come to the parched savannahs and grass begins to grow, they begin to reproduce rapidly, and become brightly colored. They gather in swarms of billions. Such a swarm can strip a field of crops in minutes, leaving the farmer with no food.

Sucking
Butterfly and moth mouthparts have evolved into a long strawlike tube, or proboscis, to enable the insect to suck liquid nectar from flowers. The proboscis is kept rolled up between feeds. The housefly (left) squirts digestive juices down its proboscis onto its food. When the food has gone mushy, the fly sucks it up.

Fly

Mosquito

Piercing
Insects such as shieldbugs and mosquitoes puncture the hard skin of plants or animals to suck out juices. Their mandibles have evolved into needlelike tubes. The insect feels for a suitable place to puncture with the soft labium which surrounds its "needle." Then it stabs its prey, and pumps in digestive fluids before it sucks the victim's juices out.

Mandibles

Wood-boring beetles
The furniture beetle lays its eggs in cracks in old, dead wood. The wood provides a food source for the larvae, whether it is a dead tree or a valuable piece of antique furniture. Undetected, the larvae, or "woodworm," tunnel through the wood, and eventually pupate. Flight holes suddenly appear in the wood as the adult insects leave to mate and lay eggs on a new food source. Flight holes have sometimes been faked in new furniture, to make it appear older, and therefore more valuable.

Insects as food
Although few people from Western countries consider eating insects, they are nutritious, and are eaten as delicacies in many parts of the world. Australian Aborigines eat adult bogong moths, and the fat "witchetty" grubs of the giant wood moth. In Africa mosquito pie is eaten, and in Asia stir-fried locust is popular.

49

THE FIRST FISHES

Fossil fishes are first recorded in rocks of Cambrian era, but preservation is quite poor. By the Ordovician, however, the fossils show enough detail for scientists to give names to the fishes. Fishes found in these rocks often had armor instead of scales and many did not have jaws. During the Devonian that followed, many new types of fishes evolved, including sharks and rays, and bony fishes. The Late Devonian also saw the evolution of *Eusthenopteron,* a fish that developed lungs and could walk on land using its strong front fins.

Crinoid

Rare cones

Nautiloids are mollusks and are related to ammonites. During the Ordovician, most had straight, cone-shaped shells, instead of the familiar coiled shells of ammonites. At the end of the Permian period, all the straight cones became extinct. The coiled cones survived, and evolved to produce a variety of ammonites.

Nautiloid

Helovites

Streptelasmid

Protective armor
Some of the Devonian fishes were completely encased in an armor made up of bony plates, while others also relied on scales for protection. The osteostracans did not have armor that covered all of the body; it was limited to the head. The placoderms were a group of armored fishes that evolved many strange shapes. Their heads and forequarters were covered with heavy armor. These species were not very successful and did not survive the Devonian. Some, like *Coccosteus,* were probably good swimmers. Not all Devonian fish had armor; thelodonts and anaspids were covered with small scales.

Ancient corals
Many rocks of the earlier part of the Paleozoic contain the remains of coral reefs. Corals are first known from the Cambrian, but it was not until the Silurian that large coral reefs became common. Two types of coral built the reefs. Colonial corals (for example *Favosites*) are made up of many animals all living in the same stony coral. Solitary corals only have one animal living in them. The reefs were home to other creatures including crinoids, nautiloids, trilobites, and fishes. Ancient corals tended to be larger than today's and lived singly, like sea anemones.

A best-seller
Hugh Miller (1802-1856) was a
stonemason from Scotland. He
collected many important fossils
from the Old Red Sandstone that
outcrops in northern Scotland. Many
were of Devonian, armored, jawless fish.
Miller is famous for a series of popular
geology books he wrote in the 1840s and
1850s. These books were
best-sellers at the time.

Alive and kicking
Coelacanths are known from
fossils in rocks ranging from the
Devonian to the Cretaceous,
when it was thought they became extinct.
In 1938, a strange fish was caught by
fishermen off the southeastern coast of
Africa. Scientists noticed the similarity
between this fish with its leglike fins (called
Latimeria), and fossils of prehistoric fish,
and decided that the coelacanths are still
alive today! *Latimeria* lives in the deep
waters of the Indian Ocean.

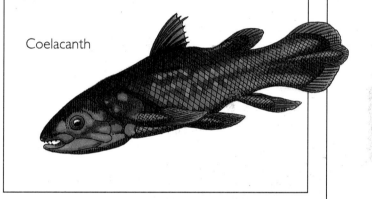

Coelacanth

Favosites

Crinoids (sea lilies),
above, are related to
starfish and sea urchins.
They attached
themselves to the
seafloor.

Jawless fish
Most of the earliest fish did not have jaws.
They belong to class Agnatha, which means
"no jaws." They had a simple hole for a
mouth and many must have grubbed about
for organic debris in the sediment under the
water. Today, there are two living groups of
agnathans, the lampreys and the hagfish. It is
thought that the class Gnathostomata (all of
the vertebrates with jaws) evolved from
jawless fish. The jaws were formed from
some of the bones that supported the gills.

Thelodonts

Osteostracans

Anaspid

Dinithys

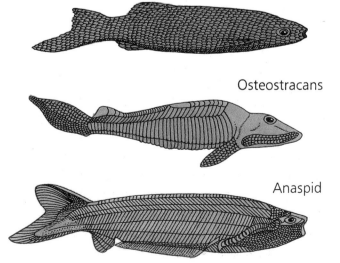

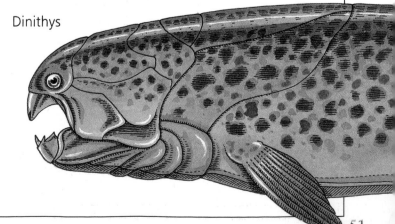

ANIMAL SHAPES

DESPITE THE GREAT variety of animal shapes in nature, all creatures need to have some way of keeping their bodies from collapsing or falling apart.

Some, called vertebrates, have an internal skeleton, made out of bone or cartilage. The skeleton is centered around a backbone. It supports the body's shape and protects the internal parts. Vertebrates include mammals, such as humans and horses, fish, such as sharks, and birds.

Others have no internal skeleton and need different ways of keeping their body shape, such as a hard outer skeleton. These animals are collectively known as invertebrates, and they include crustaceans, such as lobsters, mollusks, such as slugs, and jellyfish.

JELLYFISH
This beautiful creature has no solid skeleton to support its body. Instead, its shape is maintained by soft, water-filled inner tissues, over which its outer layers are stretched. Take a jellyfish out of water, and its body will collapse.

SLUG
As with the jellyfish, a slug keeps its body shape by stretching its skin over fluid-filled body parts. The slug, however, is not supported by water, like the jellyfish. The pressure from inside keeps its body from collapsing.

LOBSTER
The lobster is surrounded by a rigid skeleton, like a suit of armor. Although it protects the lobster, it prevents growth and is shed each time the animal grows. It is also very heavy, and makes the lobster clumsy when placed out of water.

HORSE
Like you, the horse has an internal skeleton of bone to support its body. Instead of walking on two legs, its skeleton is one of a powerful, four-legged runner, with long leg bones and large neck bones to support a heavy head.

SHARK

Sharks, such as the whale shark (left), and other related fish, including rays and dogfish, have skeletons that are made from gristle (cartilage). This substance is like bone, but more flexible. These creatures are called cartilaginous fish.

BONY FISH

Other fish have skeletons made from bone (see X ray, above). Known as bony fish, they all have a central spinal column on which the ribs, skull, and fins are anchored. The fish's muscles can pull on this framework, enabling the fish to arch its body and tail to one side and then to the other in order to swim through the water.

HUMAN

Your skeleton is made from a tough material called bone. Its shape is unique to humans, having developed over millions of years to produce an animal that can walk upright on two legs. The large skull holds a big brain with which to think. The hands can grasp objects firmly or pick up, hold, and manipulate the most delicate items.

SUPPLE, STRONG, AND MOBILE

The bones in your skeleton fulfill a number of different roles. They protect your soft internal parts as you move about and play a sport (left). The skeleton also allows your body to move, by giving the muscles levers to pull against. Bones also contain marrow which makes the tiny blood cells that flow through your veins and arteries. Finally, your skeleton acts as an important store for minerals that are needed by the body. These minerals are found in crystals that, along with fibers of collagen make up bone tissue.

WHAT ARE REPTILES?

There are probably more than 10 million different kinds, or species, of animals in the world. About 6,500 are reptiles – "cold-blooded" creatures with a bony internal skeleton and scaly skin, that breed by laying eggs. Despite their small proportion of total animal species, reptiles are one of the best-known animal groups. They include slithering snakes, speedy lizards, slow tortoises, flippered turtles, and fearsome crocodiles. Those giants of the distant past, the dinosaurs, were also reptiles.

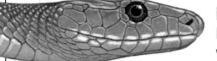

Reptile eggs

Reptiles are vertebrates – animals with backbones. Like another group of vertebrates, birds, they lay tough-shelled eggs. The shell houses and protects the baby animal as it develops inside, using the food store in the egg known as yolk. The eggs of turtles, snakes, and most kinds of lizards have tough, leathery, slightly flexible shells. Those of tortoises, crocodiles, and lizards such as geckoes have hard, brittle shells, more like a bird's egg. However, some lizards and snakes do not lay eggs. The young develop inside their mother and are born fully formed.

Hatching

Baby reptiles have a hard, horny scale on the mouth, called the egg tooth. They use it to crack their way out of the egg.

The lizard group

There are about 3,750 species of lizards, from tiny wall and sand lizards to big, sturdy monitors and iguanas. Lizards are the most widespread reptile group.

The crocodile group

There are about 22 species of crocodiles, alligators, caimans, and gavials, called crocodilians. They have powerful tails and mostly live in swamps, lakes, and rivers.

A reptile puzzle

The worm lizards are a small group of reptiles, with about 140 species. Neither worms nor lizards, they are in a reptile group of their own, called the amphisbaenids. Most have no legs and live in tropical and subtropical places, burrowing in the soil of forests to prey on worms, insects, and other creatures. The biggest amphisbaenids are 30 ins (75 cms) long.

The skeleton

The skeleton of a reptile is similar to other vertebrates, being composed of a skull, a line of bones called vertebrae making up the spinal column, and four legs. The vertebrae carry on past the hips to form the tail.

Skull

Leg bones

Main vertebrae (backbones) of spinal column

Front foot bones

Dragons galore

Myths, legends, and stories from all over the world feature dragons, sometimes called "great worms." The typical dragon is a reptile-like creature. It has scaly skin, breathes fire, flies on vast wings, guards stolen treasure, attacks humans, and is evil and cunning. One of the most famous is Smaug, the huge and terrible dragon from J R R Tolkien's exciting folk story *The Hobbit*, written in 1937.

Inside a reptile

A reptile such as this crocodile has all the main internal parts common to other vertebrate animals, like frogs, birds, or mammals such as yourself. These include a brain, heart, stomach, intestines, kidneys, and the bones of the skeleton.

The snake group

There are about 2,400 species of snakes, from tiny thread snakes to huge pythons. They have long, slim, flexible bodies, and most lack all traces of legs.

The turtle group

There are about 240 species of turtles, tortoises, and terrapins, called chelonians. Many have domed shells of bone and horn.

Snakeless zone

The island of Ireland has no snakes. Christian legend says that they were banished by Saint Patrick (389-461 A.D.), patron saint of Ireland, because they were evil. A more likely biological explanation is that snakes have never managed to spread to Ireland from mainland Britain because of the wide barrier of the Irish Sea.

CLAWS FROM THE SKY

In Medieval Europe, it happened every year, as surely as spring followed winter. The eagles came hunting the lambs. Armed only with slings and bows, there was little the shepherds could do to guard their sheep. One minute the flock would be grazing peacefully and the next – a beating of wings, a chorus of terrified bleating – and another lamb was carried off to eager beaks in a distant aerie (*main picture*).

Eagles are not always as bold and fierce as they look, however. Most will eat the easiest meal available, including carrion (dead animals). They generally avoid humans and will only attack if cornered, especially when defending their nests.

Snatch!

Daylight hunters – such as falcons (left), *buzzards, hawks, merlins, and kestrels – circle or hover above their prey, waiting for the chance to strike. Peregrine falcons drop from the sky at incredible speeds (up to 220 mph), snatching their prey with clawed talons.*

EAGLE EYES

All hunting birds have remarkable hearing and eyesight. The night-hunting owl can detect the scuffling of a mouse many feet away, and its unusual, forward-facing eyes allow it to zero in on its target with deadly precision. A single pair of owls will clear a wide area of thousands of rats and mice.

KINGS OF THE AIR

Although only a few of the 8,500 species of birds hunt living mammals, the power, speed, and grace of these creatures are awesome. The golden eagle with its 7-ft wingspan, is widely seen as the king of birds. Since ancient times, people have trained captive eagles (*left*), hawks, and falcons to hunt for them.

Poised for the Kill
Until firearms were used to scare them off, eagles were a problem at springtime (below).

Holy Hawks
All cultures respected the swift hawk (right). To the ancient Greeks and the Aztecs, it was a messenger for the gods. Some Native American peoples believed a hawk helped to create the world. The Ainu of Japan sacrificed hawks with the prayer: "Divine hawk, you are an expert hunter, let your cleverness fall on me."

A SIGN OF STRENGTH

Because the mighty eagle was thought to be able to fly nearer the sun than other creatures, and even look at it without blinking, it became a symbol of power and victory.

Not surprisingly, many peoples made it their emblem. Roman soldiers were prepared to die for their eagle standards (*left*). Russian and Austrian emperors also used eagles as their symbols, and the United States chose the bald eagle as its national bird in 1782.

PAINFUL PUNISHMENT. According to Greek legend, Prometheus was punished by Zeus, king of the gods, by being chained to a mountain and having his liver pecked out by an eagle (*right*). As his liver grew again during the night, his horrible ordeal was repeated day after day!

The Hunter Hunted
Humans have long admired birds of prey, but today many species, such as the Java hawk and the Monkey-eating eagle, are under threat as their forest homes are destroyed. Though eagles are protected in most countries, they are still hunted illegally for sport.

SPQR

IX

Although the term "avalanche" can mean the fall of any material – snow, soil, rocks, ice, or volcanic lava – it generally refers to a falling mass of snow. Dry-snow avalanches can travel at speeds of up to 225 mph. The melting snow of a wet-snow avalanche moves more slowly, at about 20 mph.

Wet-snow avalanche

Wet-snow avalanches often begin in rocky areas. Here, the snow melts around rocks that have warmed up in the sunshine. The fresh, wet snow can set as hard as concrete when the avalanche finally comes to a halt.

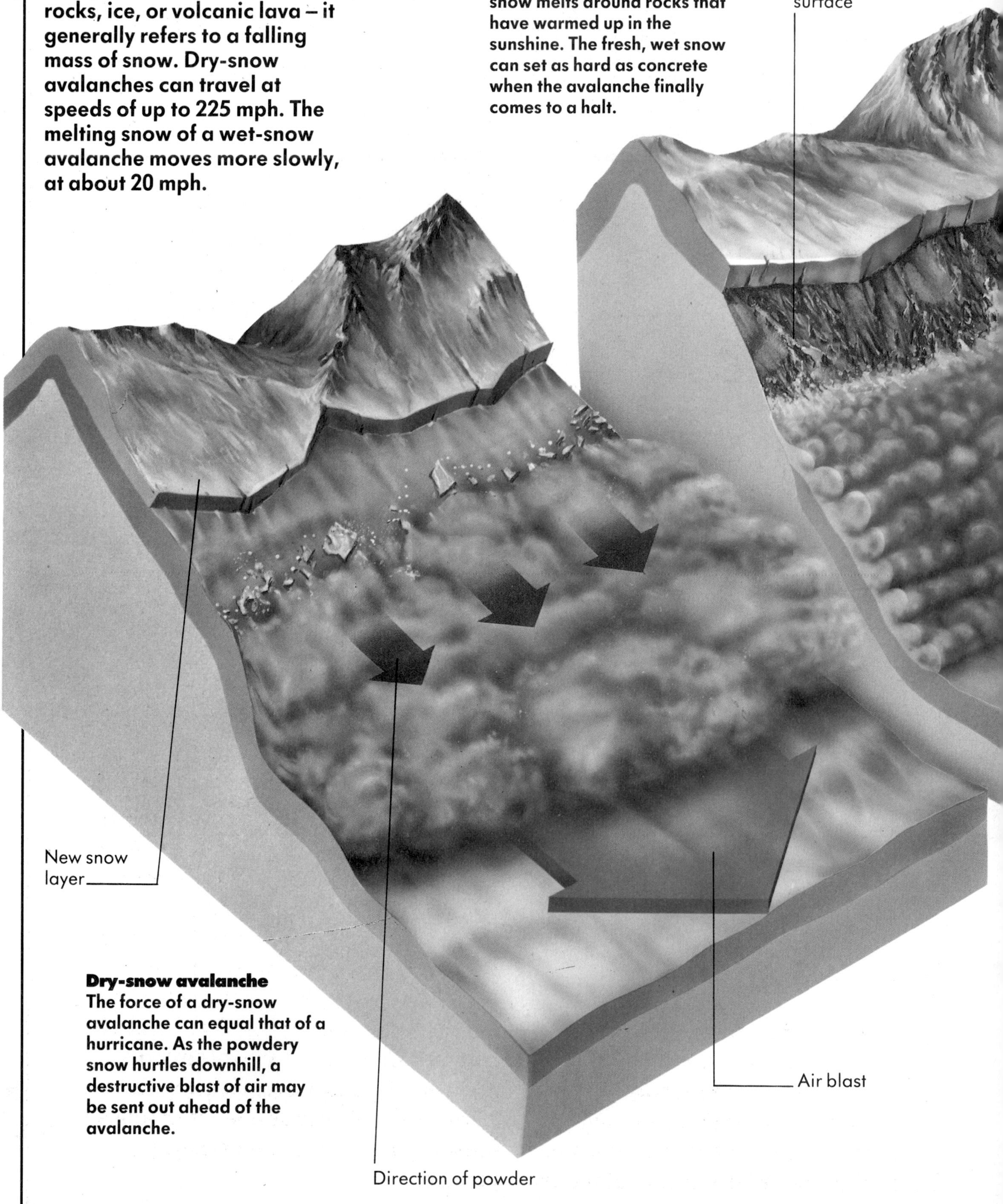

Melting snow exposes rocky surface

New snow layer

Dry-snow avalanche

The force of a dry-snow avalanche can equal that of a hurricane. As the powdery snow hurtles downhill, a destructive blast of air may be sent out ahead of the avalanche.

Air blast

Direction of powder

New snow layer

Direction of slab

Slab avalanche
As a slab avalanche hurls itself down a slope, the front of the slab starts to break up. Slab avalanches usually occur on slopes that are protected from the wind, where the snow collects in deep piles.

Snow rolls into balls

WHAT IS AN AVALANCHE?

An avalanche is a huge mass of ice and snow which breaks away from the side of a mountain and surges downward at great speed. The greatest avalanches probably occur on the high peaks of the Himalayas. However, those which cause the highest death toll fall in the populated valleys of the Alps.

Scientists have grouped avalanches into three main kinds: wet-snow avalanche, dry-snow avalanche, and slab avalanche. Wet-snow avalanches

usually occur in the spring, when the loose, melting snow forms into large boulders of snow as it rolls downhill. More deadly are the dry-snow avalanches, which either slide along close to the ground, or lift off the ground completely and swirl through the air, often hundreds of feet high. In a slab avalanche, a huge chunk of solid, sticky snow breaks away from a slope. It slides across a layer of loose snow crystals lying beneath the surface.

ANTS AND TERMITES

Ants belong to the group of Hymenoptera, like bees and wasps. Termites belong to the order of Isoptera, meaning equal wing. Nevertheless, ants and termites have very similar life-styles. They are mainly social insects, living in huge families or colonies, where each insect has a particular job to do. Most do not reproduce; their lives are devoted to caring for their sisters and brothers. Only the queen mates and lays eggs. Her many young, the workers, build, repair, and defend the nest.

Caste of thousands
Different kinds, or castes, of ants or termites perform different jobs in a colony. Worker ants tend the queen (left), the grubs, and pupae (right). Others clean the nest (above right) and go out in search of food. Soldiers defend the colony.

Queen ant

Workers

Pupae

Social ants

Most ants have poor eyesight, but a good sense of smell. They communicate with nest members through touch and through scents called pheromones which they produce. When foraging ants find food, they lay a scent trail for others to follow. Worker ants produce a different scent if they find a damaged part of the nest, which brings others to help with the repair. Ants from one colony recognize each other by their smell, and will attack an intruder from a different colony. They defend themselves by biting and squirting stinging formic acid into the wound they have made. Ants feed on many different types of food. A column of army ants will tear apart and carry off any small creature in its path. Each ant can lift a load many times its own weight.

Making an ant home
You can study ants more easily by building an ant home from a glass tank or plastic box. Cover the outside of the tank with dark paper. Half-fill the tank with earth, and stock it with small black or red ants from the garden. Add damp soil and leaves. After a few days, remove the paper, to see the tunnels built against the sides.

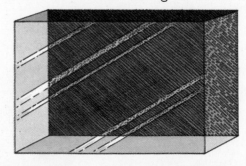

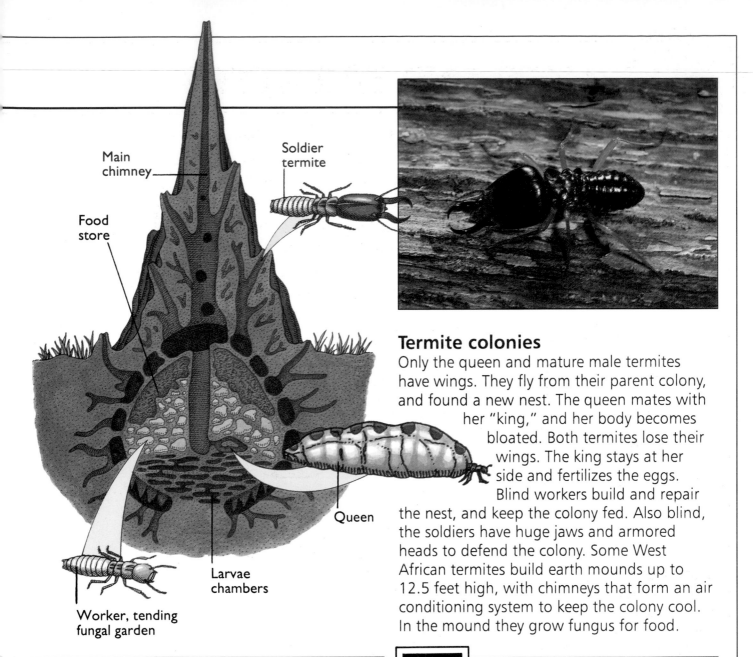

Main chimney

Food store

Soldier termite

Queen

Larvae chambers

Worker, tending fungal garden

Termite colonies

Only the queen and mature male termites have wings. They fly from their parent colony, and found a new nest. The queen mates with her "king," and her body becomes bloated. Both termites lose their wings. The king stays at her side and fertilizes the eggs. Blind workers build and repair the nest, and keep the colony fed. Also blind, the soldiers have huge jaws and armored heads to defend the colony. Some West African termites build earth mounds up to 12.5 feet high, with chimneys that form an air conditioning system to keep the colony cool. In the mound they grow fungus for food.

Feed ants on ripe fruit, meat, or jam, and provide fresh leaves and water on damp kitchen paper. Keep your tank in a cool place, and cover it when you are not studying ant behavior, so air can get in, but the ants can't escape. If you have managed to catch a large queen with your stock, the colony should go on indefinitely, and may even produce a swarm of winged ants in the summer. Let them go to produce a new nest.

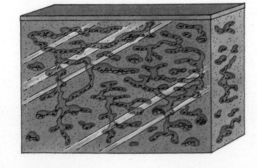

Anteaters of the world

Ants and termites are food for any animal with strong claws to rip open the nests, and a long, sticky tongue to lick the insects out. In Central and South America, armadillos and giant anteaters (below) live on the savannah, and collared anteaters are found in the forests. The aardvark lives off the same diet in South Africa, and the pangolin in Asia. The spiny anteater lives in Australia.

THE KING OF BEASTS

The year was 1900. The plan was to build a 700-mile railroad from Kampala, capital of Uganda, to the port of Mombasa on the Indian Ocean. It was a massive task, but the engineers said it could be done. Building the track soon proved the least of their worries.

At Tsavo, near the foothills of Mount Kilimanjaro, the line had to cross lion territory. The beasts objected. The man-eaters of the Tsavo killed 28 railroad workers and work stopped for weeks (*main picture*). Finally, the lions were hunted down and shot. But the local people knew exactly what had been happening: An ancient king and queen had returned as beasts to defend their territory.

Beware the Lioness
Although smaller than the male, the lioness (above) *can run faster (at 32 mph) and is more dangerous, especially if her cubs are threatened. It is she who teaches the young to hunt. A lion can kill an animal three times its own weight.*

MOTHER'S PRIDE

The largest of the cat family, a lion can weigh over 400 pounds and measure 10 feet from nose to tail. Once found from Greece to India, most lions now live in east and southern Africa, usually in family groups (called prides) of one or more adult males and several females.

Using their sharp claws and teeth (*left*), lions will eat almost any available creature, from 8,000-pound hippopotami and giraffes to grass mice and tortoises.

KING OF BEASTS. The lion, widely regarded as the King of Beasts, is often seen as the symbol of might and power. It is celebrated by the Bapende people of Kongo (*left*), is the destroyer of demons in Hinduism, the defender of the law in Buddhism, and is featured in many coats of arms, particularly that of British kings and queens.

Sacred Cats

To the people of South and Central America the jaguar is the Master of Animals. Mayan rulers were said to be descended from jaguars, and the elite Aztec jaguar warriors were dressed as them (above right). Today the jaguar symbol is used by a car manufacturer (right).

Traditional African priests wear leopard skins. Peoples who believe the beast is holy may not eat its flesh because it helps the spirits of the dead.

Spot the Leopard?

Though the leopard (left) weighs just 154 lb, it is a far more cunning predator than the lion. It hunts alone at night, and has been known to drag away human victims without waking up other people living in the same house.

TEAM HUNTERS

Healthy lions feed off grazing animals, such as gazelles. They hunt together, stalking their prey downwind and striking with sudden speed and ferocity. However, even working in packs, only one in five hunts ends in a kill.

Lions' eyes are designed for seeing at night, and most hunts occur just after dark or before sunrise. Older beasts, with failing teeth and strength, may acquire a taste for human flesh, but attacks on people are not common.

WHAT IF FISH COULD FLY?

Most fish move by swimming through the water, either by wiggling their body from side to side, or by waving their fins. A few have learned how to use their fins to walk on land. Other fish have developed the ability to leap from the water and swoop and glide above the surface for several feet, before plunging back down into the waves. They are called flying fish.

Take off
If they are threatened by a predator, such as a shark, flying fish will gather speed, up to 20 mph (32 km/h), and shoot above the waves.

What if you could ride a sea horse?

Sea horses are true fish, cousins of pipefish and sticklebacks, but with a very strange body shape. The face resembles a horse's head, with small pectoral fins sticking from the neck, one dorsal fin on the back of the stiff body, and a curly tail to wrap around plants or rocks to hold the fish in place. Instead of getting forward movement by swishing its tail, the sea horse waves its dorsal fin very quickly to move itself forward. By swimming at a modest speed, the sea horse can suck or snap any food into its small, tube-shaped mouth.

Swooping to safety

Once the flying fish becomes airborne, it can glide for more than 330 feet (100 m) and up to 20 seconds on its outspread pectoral fins. This will take it far away from any danger.

Flapping fish

The freshwater hatchetfish of South and Central America (above) is able to fly through the air by rapidly flapping its pectoral fins, in much the same way as a bird flies.

How to swim

Although all fish swim, they don't all swim in the same way. The majority of fish, such as tuna and sharks, get the power for their forward movement from their tails, or caudal fins. Fish also need a variety of other fins around their body to control their movements. Dorsal fins keep the fish upright, while steering and braking are provided by the pectoral and the pelvic fins.

Tuna swim at more than 44 mph (70 km/h) by moving their tail from side to side. The front of the body remains fairly still.

Caudal fins

Dorsal fins

Pelvic fins

Pectoral fins

Sharks and dogfish swim by swinging their tail from side to side, while the rest of the body curves in the opposite direction.

Eels move through the water by bending their body in curves, like a snake.

REPTILE SCALES

One of the typical features of a reptile is its scaly skin. On most reptiles the scales are numerous, small, and overlapping. Like a suit of armor made from linked chain mail, they form a tough but flexible covering over almost the entire body. This allows the reptile to bend its body and limbs, so that it can move about. At the same time, the scales give good protection against drying out, and from the teeth and claws of enemies. In most reptiles, the scales are replaced singly or in patches as they wear. In snakes, however, the whole skin is usually shed at once, a process called sluffing.

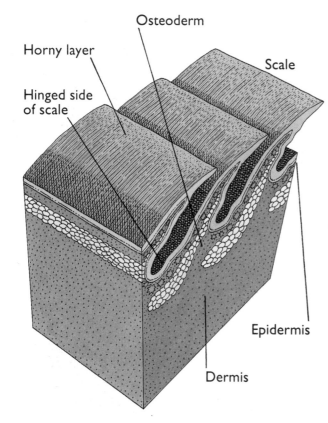

Osteoderm

Horny layer

Scale

Hinged side of scale

Epidermis

Dermis

Scale structure

Each reptile scale is made of a hard, horny material called keratin, the same substance that forms your own nails. The scale is a thickened plate of keratin set within the outer skin layer, or epidermis. It has a flexible hinge area along one side, so that it can tilt and twist slightly when the animal moves. In crocodiles and many lizards, there are additional plates of bone called osteoderms, set deeper in the skin. These strengthen and reinforce the scale layer above. Below is the dermis, containing blood vessels and nerves.

Useful skins

Since prehistoric times, people have used the tough, strong skins of reptiles for many purposes. They made the skins into hard-wearing purses, belts, boots, shoes, and coats. The colors and patterns of reptile skins are very beautiful. In some countries people believe that they gain strength by wearing the skin of a powerful animal such as an alligator. However, the reptile skin trade caused many species to become rare. Today it is controlled by laws.

New skin for old

As with your skin, reptile scales wear away. They are replaced as cells in the base of the epidermis multiply, forming new scales. When sluffing its skin, a snake rubs itself against rocks and twigs to pull off the old layer, revealing the ready-formed skin beneath.

Suits of armor

Through the ages, people have tried to make suits of armor that give the same all-over protection as reptile scales. However, the armor was rarely as light or as flexible as the natural reptilian version. In Europe, suits of armor were made from plates of metal, as shown here. In China and Japan, it included sheets of thick leather. Perhaps the most effective armor was chain mail, formed from small metal rings looped together.

The gila monster is a lizard with curious rounded, bead-shaped scales.

The armadillo lizard has big, spiky scales for protection and can roll into a ball to defend itself from predators.

The rattler's rattle

The poisonous rattlesnake shakes its tail rattle very fast to make a buzzing or rattling noise, that warns other animals to keep away. The rattle is formed from large tail scales that have remained behind when previous skins were shed. The scales are linked loosely together, the bent-over end of one fitting into a circular groove in the next. There is a story that the longer the rattle, the older the rattlesnake. However, scales sometimes break off the rattle by accident. So rattle length is only a rough guide to the snake's age.

Basal scale

Terminal scale

Loose link between scale

WHERE BIRDS LIVE

With their adaptations for flight and feeding, birds are able to live all over the world. They range from the freezing Poles to the baking deserts, and from rushing rivers to steamy jungles. Flight has given them the mobility to exploit a wide variety of food supplies and habitats. Being warm-blooded, they also have the advantage of maintaining a constant body temperature and staying active whatever the weather.

Antarctica

The 16 species of penguin all live in the Southern Hemisphere. Six species, including these emperor penguins, are even found in Antarctica itself, despite the extremely cold temperatures and wind. Emperors are the largest of all penguin species. They grow to about three feet (1 m) tall.

The tropics

About two-thirds of all species of birds live in the world's tropical rain forests. They include trogons and parrots. Rain forest birds are often brightly colored. The bright green feathers of this rainbow lorikeet blend in with the foliage. Even its colorful markings could be mistaken for flowers or fruits in the lush forest.

Bird-watching

The best places to observe birds are parks, gardens, or wooded areas. Sit very quietly and try to keep out of sight. In a forest you will see that different species prefer a particular part of the woods. Some birds will feed on the ground, others might nest among shrubs, and some will sing from tree branches. Watch patiently and note down the colors, shape, and behavior of different types of birds, and where and when you saw them.

Desert

Roadrunners live in the North and Central American deserts. They rarely fly, but can race at great speeds after their prey – insects, lizards, and snakes. They survive the scorching heat of the desert by staying in the shade until dusk, when the air and ground cool off.

Mountains

Some birds of prey, like this golden eagle, soar above high mountains. They glide on rising currents of air, keeping a lookout for prey below. They nest on cliff faces where they can rear their eaglets, protected from predators.

Never disturb nests or harm birds or eggs.

Keep a scrapbook to record the birds you see. Later you can compare it with a bird identification book.

National birds

Birds can be found virtually all over the world. Many nations have adopted as symbols birds that are native to the country or which migrate through the region. Often they are chosen for their beauty, rarity, or some other special feature. Some birds have even been incorporated onto national flags or emblems. Try to think of other ways in which birds have been used as symbols.

Australia

The black swan of Australia is revered as it is one of only three swan species in the Southern Hemisphere. It is all black with white wing feathers and a red bill.

Papua New Guinea

The flag of this country carries the silhouette of a bird of paradise, which is native to New Guinea. These birds are famed for their dazzling plumage and courtship displays.

The United States

The bald eagle was adopted as the national emblem of the United States in 1782. It was chosen because it is such a powerful, noble-looking bird.

Egypt

Egypt's national flag shows a bird of prey, which symbolizes strength. Kestrels were held sacred in Ancient Egypt, and were often mummified.

Uganda

The national flag of Uganda in East Africa shows an African balearic crane, also known as a crowned crane. They are residents of this region and are held in special regard because of their striking appearance and amazing dance.

POISONOUS SNAKES

There are nearly 2,400 species of snakes around the world. But only about one-sixth of these have venom (poison) strong enough to harm other creatures. Only a few dozen have venom powerful enough to seriously harm or kill a person. Poisonous snakes use their venom to paralyze or kill their prey. Occasionally they will bite in self-defense, for example, if a careless person treads on them. Just in case, it is best to treat all snakes with respect, and to take great care when walking in places where snakes live.

COBRA

Venom gland

Fixed front fangs

Front fangs hinge forward to strike

VIPER

Venom

BOOMSLANG

Venom gland

Grooved fangs

Venom and fangs

Snake venom is made in venom glands on either side of the head. The snake injects its venom into the victim when it bites, using its long teeth, called fangs. Back-fanged snakes such as the deadly boomslang and the twig snake have grooved fangs at the rear of the mouth. Cobras, including coral snakes, have fangs at the front. Vipers, including adders, sidewinders and rattlesnakes, have long, hinged fangs that fold back when not in use.

Snake charming

In some parts of the world people "charm" snakes by playing flute music, as the snake sways to and fro, as though dancing or hypnotized. Often poisonous snakes such as cobras are used, though they sometimes have their venom glands or fangs removed. In fact, the snake can hardly hear the flute. It may react to the rocking body of the charmer and to the vibrations from his or her tapping foot.

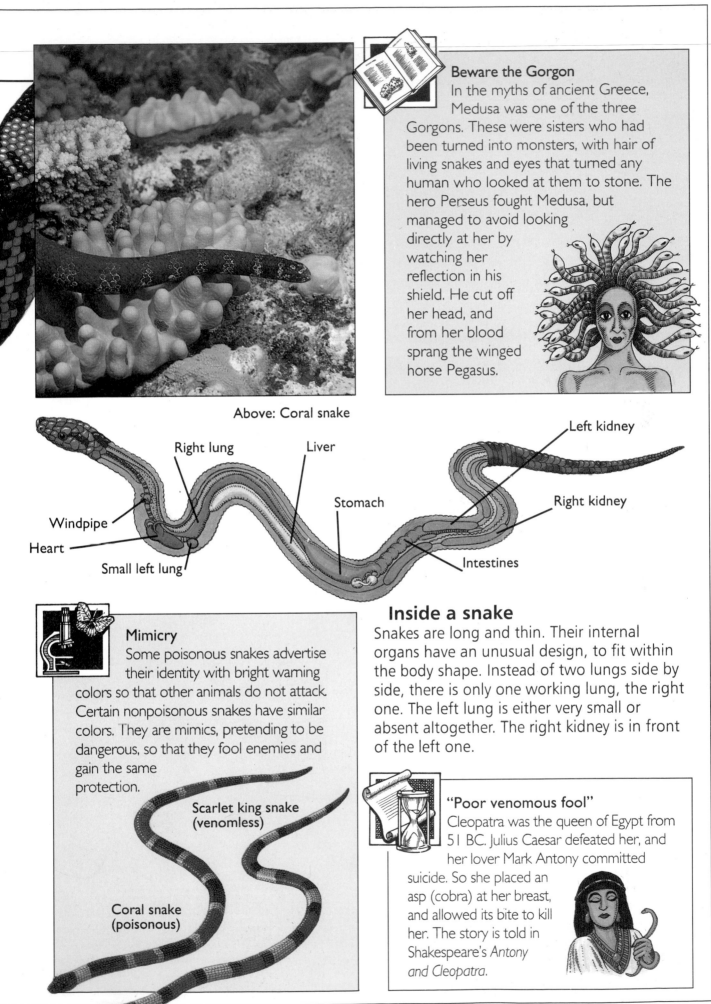

Above: Coral snake

Beware the Gorgon

In the myths of ancient Greece, Medusa was one of the three Gorgons. These were sisters who had been turned into monsters, with hair of living snakes and eyes that turned any human who looked at them to stone. The hero Perseus fought Medusa, but managed to avoid looking directly at her by watching her reflection in his shield. He cut off her head, and from her blood sprang the winged horse Pegasus.

Left kidney

Right lung   Liver

Stomach

Right kidney

Windpipe

Heart

Small left lung

Intestines

Inside a snake

Snakes are long and thin. Their internal organs have an unusual design, to fit within the body shape. Instead of two lungs side by side, there is only one working lung, the right one. The left lung is either very small or absent altogether. The right kidney is in front of the left one.

Mimicry

Some poisonous snakes advertise their identity with bright warning colors so that other animals do not attack. Certain nonpoisonous snakes have similar colors. They are mimics, pretending to be dangerous, so that they fool enemies and gain the same protection.

Scarlet king snake (venomless)

Coral snake (poisonous)

"Poor venomous fool"

Cleopatra was the queen of Egypt from 51 BC. Julius Caesar defeated her, and her lover Mark Antony committed suicide. So she placed an asp (cobra) at her breast, and allowed its bite to kill her. The story is told in Shakespeare's *Antony and Cleopatra*.

SEASONS

A season is a time of year with a particular kind of weather. Each season has a different effect on plant and animal life. Areas around the poles have only two seasons – six months of summer, when it is light nearly all the time, and six months of winter, when it is dark most of the time. Places near the equator have less defined seasons. Often there are only two, one wet and one dry. It is hot all year round, and the length of the day stays the same all year. Temperate regions between the equator and the poles, have four seasons – spring, summer, fall, and winter. The days are longer in summer and shorter in winter.

Life in the fall and winter

During these seasons, the weather may turn cooler, wetter, and more windy. There is little food for animals to eat. Some gather stores of food in the fall to help them survive the winter. Plants also rest over the winter when it is too cold for them to grow and water in the soil is frozen. Areas closer to the equator remain warm.

People in the north-east of Brazil (above) can still spend time on the beach, even in the winter.

Winter in Canada (above) often brings snow.

Seasonal festivals

In the northern hemisphere, the Christian festival of Easter happens in springtime. Easter symbols, such as spring flowers and eggs, represent new life and the resurrection (or rising from the dead) of Jesus Christ. Some Hindu festivals are connected with the annual cycle of the seasons. Pongal, or Sankranti, marks the end of the south-east monsoon and the reaping of the harvest. Beautiful kilars (decorative designs) are traced on floors with moistened rice flour.

عيد مبارك

Life in spring and summer

Spring in temperate climates brings warmer weather and the days get longer. Day and night are almost the same length. The warmth and spring showers encourage plants and trees to grow and buds to burst open. Many animals have their young in spring so that they will have time to grow strong enough to survive the cold autumn and winter seasons. Summer in the Mediterranean climate of Spain is very hot and dry. Olive trees (top left) are suited to this environment, and olive groves flourish.

Summer in Southeast Asia (above) and parts of eastern Africa can be very wet when the monsoon rains arrive between April and July.

Hibernation and migration

To survive cold, hot, or dry seasons, animals may move away or migrate to warmer, cooler, or wetter places. The arctic tern migrates from one end of the world to the other and back again, covering about 25,000 miles a year. But other migrations, such as that of the wildebeest on the African grasslands, are over much shorter distances. Instead of moving away, other animals, such as dormice, stay put and go into a deep sleep in a safe place. This behavior is called hibernation in a cold climate and aestivation in a hot climate.

Dormouse

Arctic tern

Spring bud

The four seasons

The Italian composer, violinist, and conductor Antonio Vivaldi (1678-1741) wrote four famous violin concertos called "The Four Seasons" in about 1725. Each one consists of three pieces which convey the characteristics of each season. It is one of Vivaldi's best known compositions. Vivaldi wrote nearly 50 operas, church music, and hundreds of concertos for almost every instrument known at the time.

WHAT IF A LION HAD NO PRIDE?

It would be very lonely. Lions are the only cats that live in groups, or prides. As with any group of animals, each of the lions has a different role. The females hunt for food and bring up the babies, or cubs. The males defend the females of the pride and the area of land where they live, called the *territory*, from rival males and other prides of lions.

Solitary cats

Apart from the lion, all 34 other kinds of cats – from tigers to wildcats – are mainly solitary. They live and hunt alone. Only during the breeding season when a male and a female are together, and when a mother is with her cubs, do these cats have any company.

Elephants on parade

When moving from place to place, elephants may walk in a long line, like soldiers on parade. The herd is led by the oldest female, or cow, the matriarch. The rest of the herd, including her sisters, daughters, and their babies, rely on her to find food and water.

Rival male

A fully grown male will leave his original pride. He will then wander alone for a while, then try to join another pride, so that he can mate with the females, and father offspring. But first he must challenge the pride's leader.

Leader of the pride

The chief male of the pride defends his females and territory fiercely. He fluffs up his mane to look large and strong, and growls loud and long. He tries to repel the rival by fright first. If this doesn't work, it may come to a real fight!

Female hunters

The older, experienced females are the pride's main hunters. They work together to chase and separate a herd of zebra and wildebeest, then they run down a young, old, or sick member. However, they will let the pride-leading male eat first.

Safety in numbers

Many large plant-eating mammals form herds with others of their kind. Sometimes they form mixed herds too, like zebra with wildebeest and gazelles. These herds can number from a handful to many thousands of animals.

There are many noses and pairs of eyes and ears that can detect any approaching danger. If one herd member spots trouble, it can warn the others. Should a predator approach too closely, the herd panics and runs. The hunter then finds it hard to single out one victim from the blur of bodies, heads, legs, and stripes that flash past very quickly.

Trooping baboons

The baboon is a type of monkey that spends much of its time on the ground. Baboons dwell in groups called *troops*, which can be subdivided into bands, clans, and family groups. The troops can number up to 250 baboons. These are based around the mothers and their children. There are a few males, and the biggest, most senior of these lead the troop from danger or defend it against predators, such as the leopard.

Lion cubs

Females with young cubs guard their offspring and feed them on mother's milk. However, danger may come with a rival male, which will kill any existing cubs if it takes over the pride so that its own can be reared.

Young males

The growing males stay with the pride, as long as they do not threaten the leading male. When they want to have any cubs of their own, then they must either challenge the leading male, or leave and take over another pride.

DINOSAUR PLANT-EATERS

Most dinosaurs were plant-eaters. These included the long-necked, long-tailed sauropods, which were the biggest land animals of all time; they could grow up to 20 times the size of an elephant! Then there were the armored dinosaurs: the plate-backed stegosaurs, the bone-headed pachycephalosaurs, the horn-faced ceratopsians, and the armored ankylosaurs. Some of these may have looked extremely fierce, but they were plant-eaters. The two-legged ornithopods, like *Iguanodon* and the crested, duckbilled dinosaurs, also ate plants and leaves from bushes and trees; this is called browsing. They did not graze since there was no grass. Grasses came on the scene only 25 million years after the dinosaurs had died out.

Iguanodon

The second dinosaur to be named was *Iguanodon*, in 1825. Mary Ann Mantell found some teeth of a plant-eating dinosaur in Sussex, England in 1822. Later, her husband, Gideon Mantell, found more bones and realized that they all came from the same animal. He thought the teeth looked like those of an iguana, a modern plant-eating lizard, even though they were 100 times bigger! So, he invented the name *Iguanodon*, which means "iguana tooth."

Teeth

Plant-eating dinosaurs had a variety of kinds of teeth. The giant sauropods like *Apatosaurus* had long pencil-shaped teeth with sharp edges, useful for cutting large quantities of soft leaves. Most of the armored dinosaurs, like *Ankylosaurus,* had leaf-shaped teeth with zigzag cutting edges, specialized for chewing tougher leaves.

Fossilized droppings can tell us exactly what dinosaurs ate. Sometimes they contain seeds, or leaves, or even bits of bone and fish scales.

Stegoceras

Dinosaur biomechanics

One of the best ways to understand how dinosaurs worked is to think of them like buildings or machines. *Paleontologists* (people who study fossils) may use the principles of engineering in their studies. For example, the huge sauropods had skeletons built like suspension bridges. The massive belly was held up by great ropelike ligaments, fixed to the high spine over the shoulders and hips.

Suspension bridge

Sauropod skeleton

Apatosaurus

Protoceratops

Ankylosaurus

Bleak House

Charles Dickens (1812-1870), the famous Victorian novelist, included dinosaurs in his *Bleak House*, published in 1853. Dickens wrote of meeting "a Megalosaurus, forty feet long or so, waddling like an elephantine lizard up Holborn Hill" in London. This was the same year that Richard Owen's life-sized dinosaur models were exhibited in London. Dickens had worked as a newspaper reporter earlier in his career and his books were noted for their social commentary and use of current themes of the time.

SQUID

WHAT DO THE FOLLOWING animals have in common? Land snails, pond snails, sea snails like whelks and periwinkles, cone shells, slugs, oysters, clams, scallops, and mussels. They're all mollusks! They're also called "shellfish" because their fleshy, flexible bodies are protected by a hard shell. Except, that is, for this one – the squid.

SHELL
The squid's need for speed means a heavy shell would just hold it back. Instead, there's a thin, light shell (called a pen) inside the body. Washed up on the shore after death, it looks like clear plastic.

INK SAC
If a predator comes near, the squid can squirt a dark-colored liquid from its ink sac, out of its anus. This clouds the water and hides the squid – with luck, just long enough to make a quick getaway.

STOMACH

LIVER

HEARTS

GILLS

BRAIN

EYES
Big enough to see you with! The squid and its close relations, octopus and cuttlefish, rarely bump into things. They have large eyes and excellent sight, for spotting prey, enemies, or a breeding partner.

BEAKLIKE MOUTH

SUCKERS

ARMS
There are two long arms and eight shorter ones, with suckers for grabbing prey. This is torn up by the beaklike mouth in the middle of the arm bases.

ANATOMY AT WORK
SQUIRT POWER
A mollusk's body is wrapped in a cloaklike, fleshy part, called the mantle. Between this and the main body is a mantle space. A squid sucks water slowly through a large opening into the mantle space, then squirts it out through a small funnel opening, and water streams away – backward.

LOBSTER

*L*IMBS ARE VERY IMPORTANT. They can help some animals walk, run, flap, kick, grab, push, pull, even breathe! The huge animal group called arthropods get their name from their "jointed legs." They include lobsters and other crustaceans, shown here, as well as insects, spiders, and centipedes.

CRUSTACEAN COUSINS
The big and varied crustacean group includes crabs, prawns, shrimps, crayfish, krill, barnacles, water fleas, and sand hoppers. The only ones that live on land are wood lice (sow bugs). Even they need damp places, to keep their breathing gills moist. A dry crustacean is a dead crustacean!

STOMACH

HEART

MUSCLES

BLADDER

MUSCLES

LIVER

GILLS
These are shaped like feathery flaps, and are used for breathing. There are lots of them to absorb as much oxygen from the water as possible.

PINCERS
The big pincer is mainly for crushing food, while the smaller, sharper one is for cutting.

LEGS
The lobster has ten proper jointed legs. But the first two are its big pincers. The other eight have claws on the end, to grip slippery seabed rocks.

BLOOD
The lobster's well-developed blood system has a powerful heart and lots of vessels. And its blood is blue!

SMALL MAMMALS

Most mammals are quite small. The most successful mammal group, with more species than any other, is the rodent group. Rodents are intelligent, adaptable animals with high reproductive rates. One quarter of all mammal species are bats. The smallest mammal of all is the tiny Kitti's hog-nosed bat which weighs only $1/20$ oz. The earliest placentals were insectivores. They are secretive night-time or underground animals.

Rodents and Insectivores

Beavers, squirrels, gophers, mice, rats, voles, hamsters, dormice, porcupines, guinea pigs, and mole-rats are all rodents. They are opportunists who make the most of whatever is available. They are found in every habitat, from lemmings under the Arctic snow to gerbils in the parched desert. Rabbits are not rodents, but are closely related. Long-snouted tenrecs, moles, shrews, and hedgehogs are insectivores.

Rats!
Bubonic plague is caused by a bacterium that infects rat fleas. People get the plague from flea bites and spread the disease when they sneeze. Infected people suffer fever and swollen lymph nodes (called buboes) and soon die. Epidemics have killed millions of people. In the 14th century, belongings were burned in an attempt to control the disease.

A Winter's Tale
When the weather is very cold the dormouse hibernates. First it eats large amounts of food and gets fat, then it curls up in its cosy nest. Its temperature drops to just above freezing, and its heart beat and breathing almost stop. In this state the dormouse uses very little energy and it can survive the winter.

Bats

Bats are the only mammals that can truly fly. Bat wings are formed from skin stretched over extended arm and hand bones. Most bats are nocturnal, and hide away by day in roosts. They feed on flying insects which they find in the dark. They make very high-pitched squeaks, that humans cannot hear. They can work out where the insect is from the time it takes the echo of the squeak to return, after bouncing off the insect.

Nocturnal Animals

Many small mammals are nocturnal. They come out only at night when predators that hunt by sight cannot see well. They also avoid competition with daytime animals that feed on the same food. In very hot, dry places, animals like gerbils stay hidden in dark, damp burrows in the day, coming out only at night when it is cool. Nocturnal animals, such as the urban fox (right), have well-developed senses of smell or touch to find their way around.

Animal Sizes

The African elephant stands 13 feet high and weighs six tons. Its heart beats 25 times a minute to pump enough blood for its ponderous movements. The pygmy shrew is only two inches long and weighs just two grams. It hardly ever stops scampering about and its tiny heart beats over 800 times every minute.

Wind in the Willows

These charming stories about the antics of the small mammalian friends Mole, Water Rat, Badger, and the rather pompous but loveable amphibian, Toad of Toad Hall, were first written by Kenneth Grahame as a series of bedtime stories for his son Alastair. The full collection of stories, called *The Wind in the Willows*, was published in 1908.

THE HORROR OF TAMBORA

The global weather changes caused by Tambora's eruption in 1815 inspired one of the great modern horror stories! Writers Percy and Mary Shelley and Lord Byron were staying at Lake Geneva, when the weather became oddly cold and dark for the time of year. Forced to stay indoors, they told ghost stories to suit the eerie mood and this inspired Mary Shelley to write her book Frankenstein *(right). Volcanoes erupt in different ways; Tambora was the most violent kind, in which clouds of hot gas, steam, and rock blast out from the volcano's crater (left).*

MOUNT PELÉE: NUCLEAR-FORCE EXPLOSION

In 1902, Mount Pelée in Martinique exploded with the force of a nuclear bomb. A super-heated cloud of gas and ash burst out of the side of the mountain, engulfing the town of St. Pierre in fire. Three minutes later, the town ceased to exist. Of its 30,000 inhabitants, only a handful survived (below). The ships in the harbor sank; their passengers and crews boiled alive in the water.

When Krakatoa erupted in 1883 (*right*), it was heard nearly 3,100 miles (5,000 km) away in Australia.

The ancient Roman city of Pompeii was overshadowed by a huge volcano, Vesuvius. When this erupted in 79 A.D., the whole city and its inhabitants were covered by 25 ft (8 m) of pumice and ash, which hardened around the bodies like wet cement, and created statuelike casts. These show the people at the moment of death, trying to protect themselves.

Active volcanoes almost seem to breathe... Observers of Sakura-Jima, in Japan, noticed how the volcano appeared to expand and contract as it filled up with magma (hot, melted rock).

Historic volcanoes

"The whole mountain appeared like a body of liquid fire." *Eyewitness, Tambora, 1815*

The eruption of the volcano Tambora on an island in Indonesia (*right*) was the greatest in history, and caused worldwide destruction. Light ash fell over a 400-mile (640-km) area, followed by red-hot boulders that crushed hundreds of homes. Next, red-hot volcanic ash shot high into the atmosphere and blotted out the sun, reducing temperatures worldwide. Weather conditions changed dramatically. Cold and rain ruined harvests in Europe and, in New England, snow fell in the summer, freezing laundry on the line — farmers called the year "eighteen hundred and froze to death."

Around 90,000 people died as a result of the eruption. From the start, rescue operations were ineffectual. Early explosions were mistaken for cannon fire, so the local people were not warned. The later explosions ripped the island apart, and so the governor of Java was not able to send shiploads of rice to feed starving survivors until the volcano had blown itself out over three months later. People were left to forage the few remaining edible plants.

1 The loudest explosion ever was in 1883, when the small Indonesian island of Krakatoa violently erupted.

2 As Krakatoa erupted, the island collapsed, forming a wide 4-mile (6.5-km) underwater caldera (crater) and creating giant waves called *tsunamis*.

BUGS

Bugs are a particular group of insects that share a common feature: they all pierce their plant or animal food, and suck the juices with mouthparts formed into a beak or long nose, called a rostrum. The front pair of wings in many bugs is divided into two halves, a hard front part and a delicate, transparent back part. This gives the group its scientific name, Hemiptera or half-wing. Cicadas, hoppers, aphids, and scale insects are all members of the family. Bugs undergo incomplete metamorphosis, and the young look very similar to adults. Many bugs are serious pests. Some, such as aphids, devastate plants; others carry disease, such as the assassin bugs of South America.

Water measurer

Water cricket

Saucer bug

Water boatman

Water scorpion

Many kinds of bugs are found all over the world, even at the edges of the sea. Different species are adapted to their particular environment. Bed bugs hide in crevices by day, and crawl into people's beds for a blood meal at night. Ponds team with water bugs, above and below the surface, as shown here. Shieldbugs feed on the sap of plants. European species are usually camouflaged – patterned to fit in with their surroundings. Tropical shieldbugs often have bright colors and patterns, and produce foul smells to ward off attackers. Young frog hoppers produce a nasty-looking foam known as "cuckoo-spit" as protection. Tree hoppers disguise themselves as thorns.

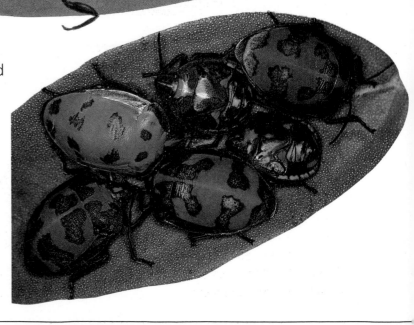

Many species of bugs live in or on the surface of fresh water. Water crickets and water measurers have water-repellent feet which do not penetrate the surface of the water. They use their feet and antennae to sense the ripples caused by a drowning insect. Once a victim is located, it is stabbed with the insect's piercing mouthparts and its juices are sucked out. Different species of water bugs prey on tadpoles, beetle larvae, and other small creatures at different depths in the water.

Insects that live underwater must still breathe air. The water boatman solves this problem by trapping a layer of air in a bubble around its body.

Virgin birth
In the spring, aphid eggs hatch into wingless females. To save time, these insects do not mate or lay eggs, but give birth to live babies. Producing young without mating is called parthenogenesis. It is quite common in insects. Later winged males and females (right) are born. They fly off to mate and lay eggs for the following year.

Great diving beetles store air beneath their wings, which can then be taken into the body through the spiracles. The water scorpion (above) has a long siphon, like a snorkel, on the end of its tail, which it extends up above the surface of the water to breathe.

Opposite page:
This group of harlequin bugs from Australia consists of three red males, a yellow female and two nymphs.

Song of the cicada
On warm summer evenings in tropical lands, in Mediterranean countries, and North America, the song of the male cicada is heard. The organ producing the sound is a "click box," like the wing mechanism located in the insect's abdomen. An area of hard cuticle is pulled in by a muscle and 'clicks' out again. Long streams of clicks are produced at different pitches. They are amplified by air sacs in the abdomen. Cicadas have ears on their abdomens so that they can hear others singing. The males sing to attract a mate. Females respond by seeking out the best singer, other males respond by singing louder.

Cuticle

Muscle

Air space

FLOWERS

The main function of a tree's flowers is to produce seeds that will grow into new trees. Flowers contain the tree's reproductive parts. They can be male or female or contain both male and female parts. Willows and poplars have male flowers on one tree and female on another. Most conifers have separate clusters of male and female flowers on the same tree. The wind carries pollen from the male flowers to fertilize the female flowers.

A flower's shape, color, and smell are designed to transfer male pollen grains to the female parts efficiently. Pollen is mainly transferred by insects or wind. Plants that rely on insect carriers have evolved brightly-colored, sweetly-scented flowers that have a landing platform for insects. In warm climates, birds and bats transfer pollen when they fly from flower to flower sipping nectar.

APPLE BLOSSOMS

Looking into flowers

Flowers vary from species to species in their shape, color, and size. Many trees in temperate (moderate, seasonal) climates are wind-pollinated, so they have unspectacular flowers because they do not rely on attracting insects.

Nikau palm flowers

Palms have small flowers which grow in large clusters. The pollinated flowers later develop into dates, coconuts, or other fruits, depending on the species.

Walnut trees grow male hanging catkin flowers 2-4 inches (5-10 cm) long. The female flowers are rounded and stand upright.

Cones of Norway spruce

Pine flowers are very inconspicuous. The red or yellow clustered flowers develop into cones about a year after being fertilized.

Walnut catkin and flowers

There are many different kinds of magnolia trees, but all are known for their beautiful flowers which lure insects.

Magnolia flowers

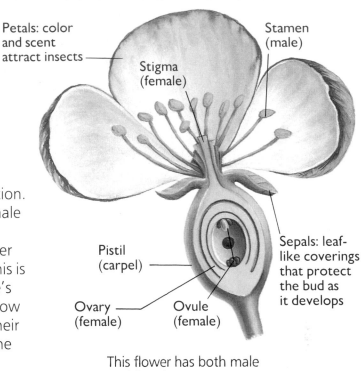

HONEYBEE

Petals: color and scent attract insects

Stamen (male)

Stigma (female)

Pistil (carpel)

Ovary (female)

Ovule (female)

Sepals: leaf-like coverings that protect the bud as it develops

This flower has both male and female parts. Stamens produce millions of pollen grains at a time, each grain is only .008 inches across.

Pollination

For a new seed to grow, male pollen grains must reach the female ovules, which are contained in the ovary. This is called pollination. Even if a flower contains both male and female parts, it very rarely pollinates itself. Pollen usually travels from the male parts of a flower to the female parts of a different flower – this is called cross-pollination. The design of a tree's flowers shows how they are pollinated. Willow catkins use the wind to carry their pollen. Their dangling shape allows the wind to scatter the pollen grains. Flowers pollinated by insects, such as bees and butterflies, attract them with their color, smell, and a store of sweet nectar to eat. Pollen sticks to the insects' legs and hairy backs, and is carried to the next flower they visit, where it may join with an ovule.

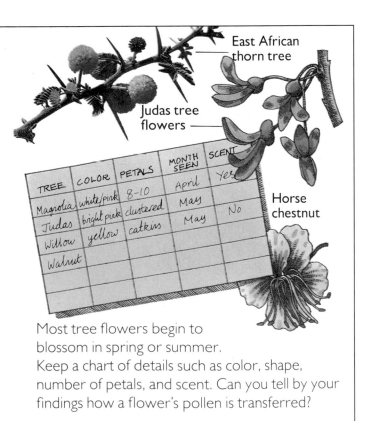

East African thorn tree

Judas tree flowers

Horse chestnut

TREE	COLOR	PETALS	MONTH SEEN	SCENT
Magnolia	white/pink	8-10	April	Yes
Judas	bright pink	clustered	May	No
Willow	yellow	catkins	May	
Walnut				

Most tree flowers begin to blossom in spring or summer.
Keep a chart of details such as color, shape, number of petals, and scent. Can you tell by your findings how a flower's pollen is transferred?

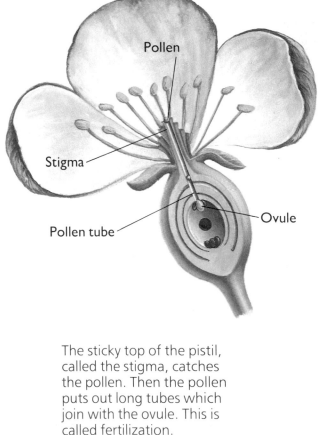

Pollen

Stigma

Pollen tube

Ovule

The sticky top of the pistil, called the stigma, catches the pollen. Then the pollen puts out long tubes which join with the ovule. This is called fertilization.

TURTLE

AMPHIBIANS LIKE FROGS must return to water to breed. Their eggs are soft and jelly-coated, and soon dry out on land. Reptile eggs don't. They have tough waterproof shells, so they can spend all their lives on land. Except those who choose to live in water, like the turtle.

SHELL
This has two layers. On the outside are thin, light scutes – curved plates made of horn (keratin). Underneath are thicker, heavier osteoderms – or plates of bone.

LUNGS
These are under the highest domed part of the shell. Some turtles can hold their breath and survive underwater for more than two hours.

BODY ARMOR
For extra strength, the scutes and osteoderms (see left) are different sizes and patterns so their joints overlap.

STOMACH

BLADDER

BRAIN IN TWO BOXES
The brain is well protected inside the thick, bony skull, which is also protected when drawn into the shell. The parts dealing with sight and smell are well developed.

BEAK
Turtles and tortoises lack teeth. They bite with the hard, sharp jaw edges. They cannot chew properly either, so food often falls out before it's been swallowed.

HEART

GUTS
A plant-eating turtle has an intestine seven times longer than its body. It is coiled into the dome of the shell.

SKELETON
The main part of the backbone is joined to the underside of the upper shell. So are some of the upper limb bones, and the ribs.

ANATOMY *AT WORK*
HOW THE TURTLE HIDES
A turtle's legs are longer than they seem. The upper parts, or thighs, are hidden in the shell, with space around each. A turtle in danger folds its legs, neck, and tail into these spaces. It also breathes out to make its lungs and body smaller, giving extra legroom.

HELLO, GORGEOUS
Turtles have good eyesight for finding prey and mates. But sometimes unnatural, human-made objects which are designed for the same purpose – protection – can trick them.

CROCODILE

REPTILES INCLUDE TURTLES AND TORTOISES, snakes and lizards, alligators, and crocodiles. The croc's gappy "smile" means death for its prey, since its bite is one of the most powerful in the animal kingdom. It drags land animals underwater, for death by drowning.

SKIN AND SKELETON
The skin has horny plates, or scutes, on it, and bony plates, or osteoderms, in it. The bones of the skeleton are strong and heavy, pulled by powerful muscles.

WINDPIPE
This tube, called the trachea, carries air into the lungs when breathing. After the oxygen is absorbed into the blood, the stale air comes back out along it.

BRAIN

BABY!

CLOSED TO DIVE
The crocodile heart has four nearly separate chambers, almost like a mammal's. When it dives, a flap inside diverts low-oxygen blood to the less-vital guts and other inner organs. The important brain and heart continue to receive oxygen-rich blood.

TWO-SPEED SWIM
A croc swims quickly by sweeping its tall, narrow tail from side to side, while holding its legs against its body. It swims slowly by kicking with its rear webbed feet, using its tail to steer.

GUTS (INTESTINE)

LUNGS

BONES

WINDPIPE

BIG BELLY
The stomach is very stretchy. It can expand to hold most of an antelope. The croc often swallows stones, which help to steady it... and may also aid digestion!

LIVER

HEART

ANATOMY AT WORK
COLD BLOOD?
Animals like reptiles are sometimes called "cold-blooded." Mammals are warm-blooded. But a crocodile basking in the sun may have blood hotter than yours! They control body temperature by basking in the sun or cooling off in the shade.

BIG, BAD WOLF?

The wolf, once common in most of Asia and Europe, is now returning to many of its old hunting grounds. It is a hunter and scavenger that sometimes operates in huge packs. Although its normal diet is small wild mammals, it has a fearful reputation because starving packs have attacked children or weakened adults. Russian wolf packs were said to have pursued sleighs to get at their terrified passengers. The gray wolf, "prairie wolf" (coyote), and Arctic wolf (*top*) were less dangerous.

What Big Teeth You Have
The wolf's jaw (below) can exert a pressure of 36 lb/in², twice that of a German shepherd dog.

HOWLING AND LAUGHING

There is no sound more certain to send a shiver down the spine than the howl of a wolf (*above*). But the wolf howl is not a signal to attack, any more than the hyena's "laugh" (*left*) means that it is enjoying itself. Wolves howl for many reasons, such as making contact, calling a pack meeting, or just out of loneliness. A howl lasts up to 20 seconds and each wolf has its own "voice."

1 2 3 4

Wolf Expressions – like humans, wolves use their faces to show how they're feeling: 1 = angry, 2 = aggressive, 3 = afraid, and 4 = terrified.

A BAD REPUTATION

The view of the wolf as a cold-blooded human killer dates from the 14th century, when the Black Death killed a third of people in Europe. Wolves were very common and probably scavenged the remains of the dead. Medieval tales like Little Red Riding Hood (*above*) spread the message: "Don't trust a wolf!"

In fact, wolf attacks on humans are very rare. Wolves will even eat worms, insects, and berries when meat is scarce.

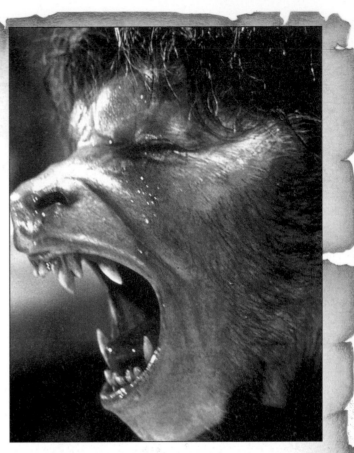

BEWARE THE FULL MOON. The myth of the werewolf was once widespread in Europe – and is still popular at the movies (such as this beast from *An American Werewolf in London*, 1983, *above*). The werewolf is a human who changes into a wolf, usually during full moon.

Native Americans greatly respected the wolf, which was often a cultural hero and the remote ancestor of some tribes. Its symbol was the Dog Star, the home of the gods.

CALL OF NATURE

American novelist Jack London (1876–1916) wrote many of the finest tales of the frozen world of the husky dog and the wolf.

The best-known are *White Fang* and *The Call of the Wild*, made into a movie in 1972 (*left*).

DINOSAUR COURTSHIP

Did dinosaurs live in families, and how did they talk to each other? How did they lay their eggs? New work in North America and in Mongolia has shown that dinosaurs were able to pass complex signals to each other, partly through sight, and partly through sound. The males and females often looked quite different from each other. The males seem to have had larger horns and crests which they may have used in fighting for mates, and for displaying, just as with deer and antelope today. After the males and females had paired off, the mothers made large nests in the ground, and laid their eggs. It seems that dinosaur societies were probably just as complicated as any mammal community today.

Males and females

Some of the biggest differences between males and females are seen among the plant-eating, duckbilled dinosaurs, like *Corythosaurus*, *Parasaurolophus*, and *Tsintaosaurus*. When many skeletons are found together, half of them may have tall crests, and the other half smaller crests. The horned dinosaurs, like *Triceratops*, also seem to show differences in the length of the horns over their eyes. The horns of the meat-eater *Ceratosaurus* may have been larger in males, who probably used them to establish territory.

Dinosaurs laid ten to thirty eggs at a time, often arranged in regular circles, in an earth nest on the ground. They covered the nest with leaves and mud to protect the eggs. After a few weeks the young hatched out. Some parent dinosaurs then fed the young after hatching.

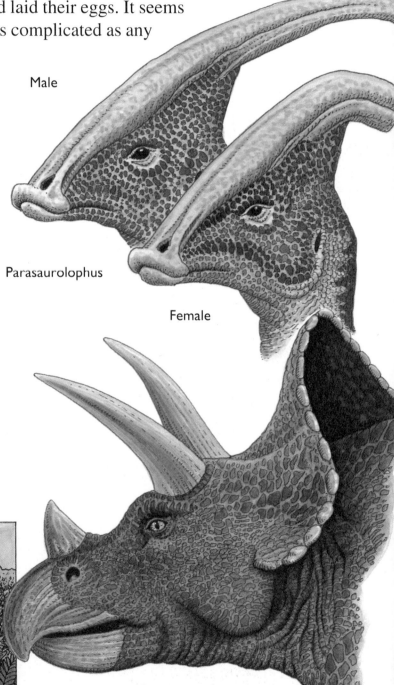

Male

Parasaurolophus

Female

Triceratops

Male birds are often brightly colored, while females are dull. The bright colors are for showing off, or displaying, for mates. Male deer have antlers for the same reasons.

Corythosaurus

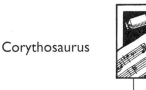

John Sibbick

One of the best-known modern dinosaur artists is John Sibbick. He painted a series of pictures of all the major dinosaurs for a 1985 book, and he is now one of the most famous dinosaur painters.

Tsintaosaurus

Musical crests

Inside the crests of the duckbills, air passages were found linking the nostrils to the throat. When air passes through a tube, it causes it to vibrate, producing sound waves. Try blowing down a long, coiled tube. This is how trumpets produce sound. When these dinosaurs puffed out hard, they whistled and produced trumpeting sounds.

Ceratosaurus

CLOUDS

Clouds are made up of millions of droplets of water or ice, which are so small and light they can float in the air. Clouds form when warm air rises. This happens when air is heated by the Sun or if it has to rise up over mountains or when cold air pushes it up from underneath. High in the sky, invisible water vapor in the air cools and turns into droplets of liquid water which gather together to make clouds. The shape, color, and height of clouds helps people to predict changes in the weather. Fog or mist are clouds that form down at ground level.

Cold front

Warm front

Cold air pushes warm air up.

Warm air slides up over cold air.

cumulonimbus – storm clouds. May rise to great heights while the bases are near the ground.

Warm and cold fronts

Clouds often form where warm air meets cold air – this is called a weather front. The cold air may push up under the warm air, forcing it to rise rapidly. This is a cold front. The passing of the front brings colder weather behind. Or the warm air may slide slowly up over the cold air, forming a warm front. Warmer weather would follow this front. In both warm and cold fronts, warm air rises, cools and may form clouds. A weather front is a sign of change in the weather, with rain and sometimes storms as a result.

cumulus – heaped-up piles of fair-weather clouds.

Heavens above

If someone asked you where heaven is, you'd probably point upward toward the sky. Throughout history, heaven has been portrayed as a spiritual place above the clouds. This illustration by Gustave Dore (1832-1883) depicts a typical heavenly scene with winged angels supported by cotton- wool clouds. Films too, such as *Matter of Life and Death* (1946) show heaven as a timeless place with expansive floors of cloud.

cirrus – high ice clouds, often first to form along a weather front.

altocumulus – sometimes referred to as a mackerel sky – sign of unsettled weather to come.

stratocumulus - not as even in thickness as a stratus.

Clouds in my coffee

When you look at the clouds, do they make you feel dreamy or sad or happy or hopeful? Clouds are quite often used to convey emotions in poetry and songs. Listen to the lyrics (words) of songs. How many can you think of that mention clouds, storms, or rain?

stratus – rain or drizzle blanket clouds

Recycling the clouds

One of the ways clouds form is when the Sun heats water on the surface of the Earth. Some of the liquid water turns to water vapor and is absorbed into the air. This change from liquid water to water vapor is called evaporation. As the warm air, which is now full of moisture, rises up into the sky, it cools down. This makes the moisture turn back, or condense, into liquid water again, forming clouds. This is called the water cycle.

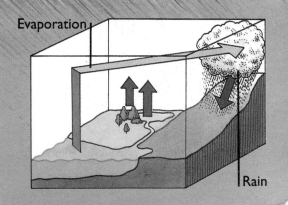

Evaporation

Rain

WHAT IF SHARKS STOPPED SWIMMING?

They would sink to the bottom and stay there. Most fish have an inner body part like an adjustable gas bag, called a swim bladder. The fish adjusts the amount of gas in the bladder to float up or down. Sharks and other cartilaginous fish lack swim bladders and can only stay up by swimming, using their rigid fins like a plane's wings.

Sharks cannot pump water over their gills, like other fish. They need to swim to get oxygen from the water into their blood. If they were to stop they would need a current of water to stay alive.

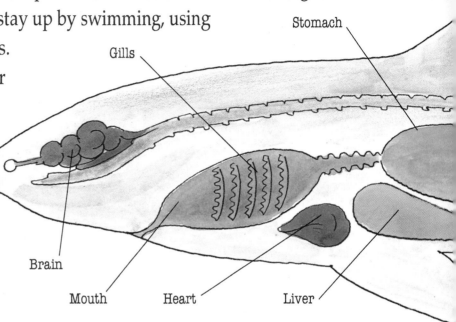

Stomach

Gills

Brain

Mouth

Heart

Liver

Which fish have wings but cannot fly?

Rays and skates are flattened cartilaginous fish. Their bodies have developed into a squashed, wing-shaped form. This is perfect for their bottom-dwelling lifestyle, where they scavenge or eat seabed creatures. While skates have a tail they can use to swim like other fish, a ray cannot swish its body from side to side, so it flaps its wings up and down to "fly" through the water.

The largest ray is the Pacific manta or devilfish. It has a "wingspan" of more than 20 feet (6 m) – about the same as a hang-glider – and weighs almost two tons. Stingrays have a sharp spine sticking out of the tail, which they can jab into enemies to inject terrible stinging poison.

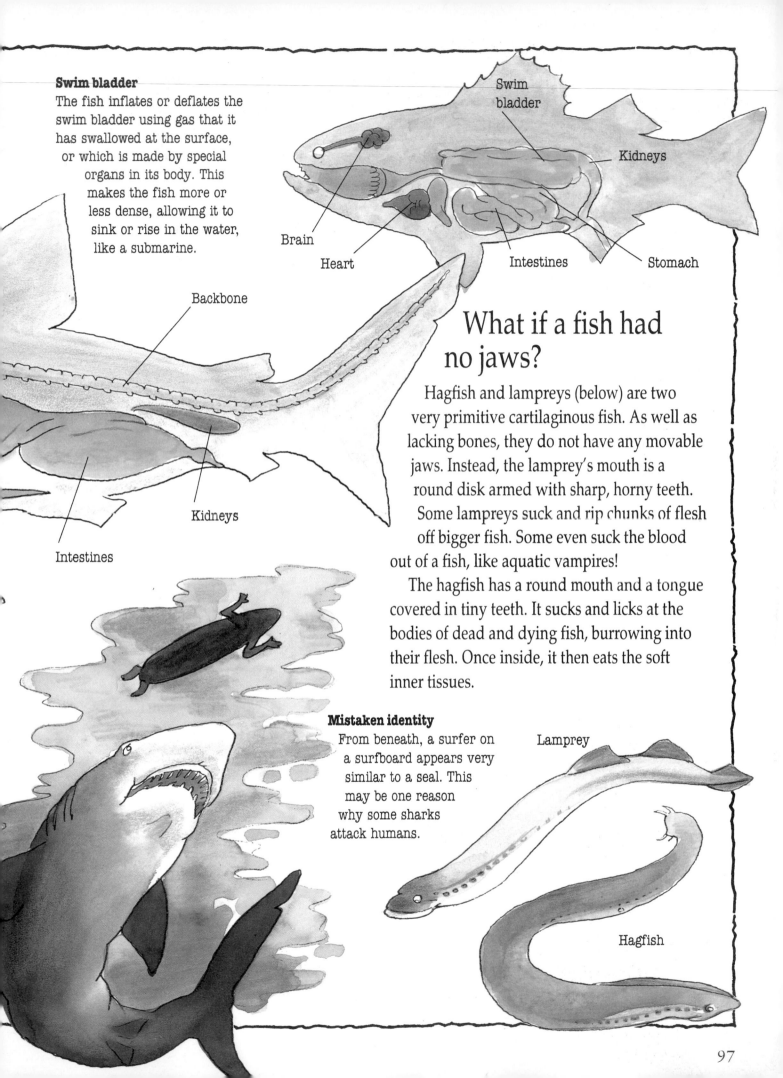

Swim bladder

The fish inflates or deflates the swim bladder using gas that it has swallowed at the surface, or which is made by special organs in its body. This makes the fish more or less dense, allowing it to sink or rise in the water, like a submarine.

Swim bladder

Kidneys

Brain

Heart

Intestines

Stomach

Backbone

Kidneys

Intestines

What if a fish had no jaws?

Hagfish and lampreys (below) are two very primitive cartilaginous fish. As well as lacking bones, they do not have any movable jaws. Instead, the lamprey's mouth is a round disk armed with sharp, horny teeth. Some lampreys suck and rip chunks of flesh off bigger fish. Some even suck the blood out of a fish, like aquatic vampires!

The hagfish has a round mouth and a tongue covered in tiny teeth. It sucks and licks at the bodies of dead and dying fish, burrowing into their flesh. Once inside, it then eats the soft inner tissues.

Mistaken identity

From beneath, a surfer on a surfboard appears very similar to a seal. This may be one reason why some sharks attack humans.

Lamprey

Hagfish

BABY MAMMALS

Young mammals do not have to fend for themselves until they are almost fully grown. Some, like mice, are born with their eyes closed, have no fur and are cared for in a cosy nest. Others, like zebra foals, are able to run with their mothers very soon after birth. All mammal babies, however, are fed on milk. Mothers, and sometimes fathers, keep their babies clean and warm, teach them the skills they will need in adult life, and protect them from predators. Baby mammals spend a lot of time playing, which strengthens their bodies and improves their co-ordination.

Multi-birth

Wolves grow up in large families. This mother wolf suckles four cubs. She provides shelter in a den and the rest of the adult pack protect them. Babies brought up in dens or nests are happy to be left alone while the mother goes out to search for food. She cannot take them with her until they are much bigger and stronger.

Number of Babies

Having lots of babies at a time is an insurance policy. Parents divide their energy between all the babies in the hope that at least one of them will survive attacks from predators (below). Having only one baby at a time is too risky; if the baby dies the parents have wasted all their energy.

Only Child

The mother sloth hangs upside down and carries her single infant on her stomach. This way she does not need to leave it alone in a den and can protect it all the time. The baby suckles for about one month, but stays put for another five months, reaching out to grab leaves as its mother slowly creeps along the branches. Eventually, it slowly wanders off on its own.

Baby Face

All parents find their babies attractive. This ensures that they will care for their young. The features of all baby mammals are similar — huge eyes set in round faces. These features often appeal to cartoonists and animators. The film *Watership Down*, about a rabbit warren endangered by human destruction, stars young rabbits who have appealing features and individual personalities.

Growth Rates

The rate at which a baby animal grows depends partly on its size. A harvest mouse is independent at 16 days — a giraffe grows for ten years. A gorilla baby also takes ten years to grow. It is much smaller than a giraffe, but it has a much bigger brain. The fastest growth rate of any baby mammal is that of the baby blue whale. During the last two months of pregnancy it puts on 220 pounds of weight daily.

The simplest family is a mother and her babies. In some cases a father is present. Elephants form stable families where babies are looked after by sisters and aunts. The leader is an old female called the *matriarch*.

Meet the family...

1. Sire Bull

2. Matriarch

3. Sisters and Aunts

4. Infant

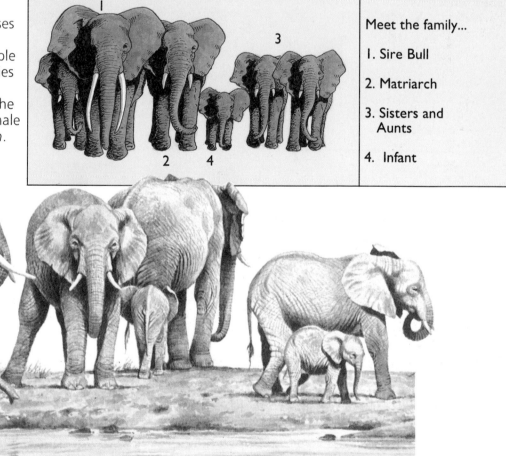

BIRD FEET

Apart from walking and running, birds also use their feet for gripping and tearing food, climbing, swimming, and preening their feathers. Most birds have three or four toes on each foot, but the exact size and shape of their feet depends on their life-style. The partridge spends most of its time on the ground, so it needs strong feet that are good for running and scratching for food. When perching birds roost on branches at night, their toes lock around the branch so they do not fall off.

For running
Ostriches have only two toes on each foot. These are highly specialized for fast running. Ostriches cannot fly, but they can run at up to 45 mph (70 km/h) for short distances.

Ostrich foot

Coot foot

For balance
The African jacana, or lily trotter, has toes about 3 inches (8 cm) long – the longest of any bird. These enable it to spread its weight over its feet so it can walk across water lily leaves without sinking.

African jacana walking on lily leaf

Mallard foot

For swimming
Ducks and geese have large, webbed feet that act as paddles when they swim, and as brakes when they land on water. Coots have lobes of skin between their toes. These help in swimming and stop the coot from sinking into mud.

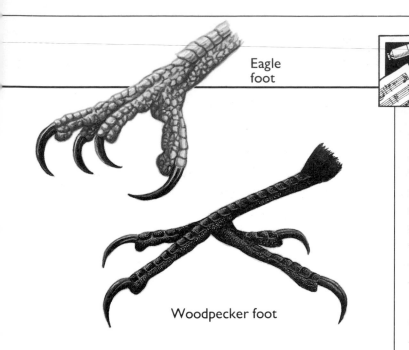

Eagle foot

Woodpecker foot

For gripping

Eagles and other birds of prey have sharp, curved talons on their feet for holding and tearing meat. Their legs and feet are very strong, but these birds find walking difficult because their talons are so long. The long-clawed feet of woodpeckers are designed for climbing tree trunks. They have two toes pointing forward and two backward.

Claws for combing

Heron claw

To keep their feathers clean and neat, birds preen them with their beaks and feet. Herons and bitterns specialize in using their feet to preen. They feed on eels, which makes their feathers slimy. To remove the slime, some of the feathers on the breast disintegrate into a powder which they rub into their dirty feathers. The heron then "combs" off the slime with tiny teeth on the middle claws of its feet. Nightjars are nocturnal birds which feed on a diet of moths and other insects. They also have comblike central claws to clean moth scales off their feathers.

Bittern claw

Great blue heron preening

Plaster casting bird prints

Before you set out to find a footprint of a bird to plaster cast, first collect the following materials: a small can, a stick, oak tag, paper clips, plaster of paris, water, clear varnish, and a knife. When you select a bird print, stand a 1 in (3 cm) wide strip of oak tag in a circle around the footprint (1). Fasten it together with a paper clip. Mix the plaster of paris in a can with water, stirring with your stick. Add water until the mixture is thick but can still be poured. Then pour the mixture into the oak tag ring, until the area is evenly covered (2). Let the plaster dry for 10 – 15 minutes. Then pry the cast loose with a knife and clean off the mud and grass. In 24 hours when the cast is completely solid, carefully clean and varnish it (3). Compare the print with a bird identification book to see if you can find out what kind of bird made it.

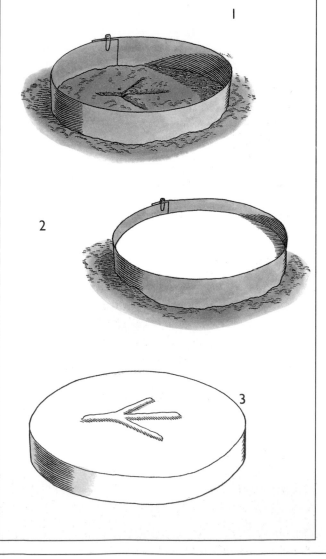

1

2

3

ARACHNOPHOBIA

Few beasts are more hated than the spider. The very sight of one paralyzes some people with terror – or sends them screaming from the room! Their fear is largely groundless. Of the 35,000 types of spiders, only a very few are dangerous to human beings.

The hairy tarantula, for example, is a shy beast whose bite is usually less painful than a wasp sting. The bite of the larger (and hairier!) "false" tarantula (*above left*) is even less venomous. Instead of despising the humble spider, we ought to thank it for feeding on genuine pests, such as germ-carrying flies and bugs.

Paralyzed with Poison
Spiders have eight legs and a front end that is head and chest combined. Some of them have eight eyes!

Spiders grab other creatures with their chelicerae (claws), paralyze them with venom, then store them in a silk picnic basket until mealtime.

Black widow

WEB SITES
Many spiders, such as the common garden spider, weave fantastic webs (*above right*) to trap their prey. Each thread is stronger than steel wire of the same thickness. Silk is made by glands in the spider's body. The silk is liquid at first but hardens into a thread when it is pulled out by little tubes called spinnerets.

Spiders living underwater spin bell-shaped webs. They fill these with air by collecting bubbles.

Danger under the Sheets
A popular scene in films is the sight of a huge spider crawling toward its victim (main picture). Such movies suggest that large spiders like the bird-eating spider (left) have a deadly bite. But the real killer is the tiny but deadly black widow spider.

Crazy Cure

The inhabitants of medieval Italy believed the bite of the tarantula drove people crazy. The only cure for their hysteria was a wild dance (right). The mythical cure stopped being used years ago – but the dance survives as the tarantella.

YARN SPINNING. Spiders are both good and bad in mythology. Christians believed it was the devil, because it trapped the innocent. The African Asanti, who had a Trickster Spider, did not think much of it either.

But the ancient Egyptians, Hindus, and Buddhists were more fond of it. Focusing on its amazing spinning, they linked it to Creation. It was the Great Weaver or the creature that drew the web of life out of itself. Native Americans believed the spider wove the first alphabet.

The Inspirational Spider

According to legend, King Robert the Bruce of Scotland failed to defeat the English six times. Hiding in a barn, he watched a spider trying to fix its web onto a beam (right). After seven attemps, it succeeded. The lesson inspired Bruce to make one more attack. The real king won a great victory at the Bannockburn in 1311.

SUPER-SPIDERS

On a desert plateau near the town of Nazca, Peru, stands the world's largest piece of art – gigantic outlines of beasts (including a 164-foot spider!) between dead-straight lines. As the monstrous shapes can only be properly seen from the air, it has been suggested that the ancient Nazcas (500 B.C. to A.D. 900) must have had balloons long before anyone else.

MUTANT HEROES. Compared with most creatures, big-brained humans are a puny lot. But all this changes in the world of fantasy, where Spider Man (*right*) slings his web and swings from one building to another, while the super-fast Wolf Man has razor-sharp claws of steel!

A firefighter burns an area of forest scrub to provide a barren area that breaks the advance of a serious forest fire.

TACKLING LARGE-SCALE FIRES

Water bombers (below) are airplanes that carry large tanks of water that can be released over a wide area of burning woodland. It takes seconds for the tank to be emptied, after which the crew takes the airplane back to the airfield to be refilled. Some types of water bombers can fly over lakes or seas to scoop up extra water.

The biggest risk of forest fires occurs following a dry spell when the wood and vegetation are tinder dry. The fires start in a number of ways: Human carelessness accounts for many, although they can also be caused by lightning or by the sun's rays magnified through discarded glass.

Hoses

Water tanks

OUT OF CONTROL

In 1997, fires raged through forests in Indonesia, encouraged by drought thought to result from a weather condition called El Niño. The whole area was clouded in thick, choking smog. The southern hemisphere was further plagued by a ring of fire around Sydney, Australia. Drought, heat, and high winds created the worst bush fire conditions in 30 years. Temperatures soared as firefighters struggled to contain the lightning-sparked blazes.

Forest fires

"It came in great sheeted flames from heaven."
A survivor describing the Lake Michigan fire, 1871

Forest fires are both terrifying and lethal. Giant flames leap from tree to tree, beneath huge clouds of smoke (*right*).

They move erratically, leapfrogging some areas to ignite the trees beyond and then returning to destroy the small islands they missed. Animals flee ahead of the pursuing wall of flames; people try to escape the heat by hiding in water tanks or wells, or by sheltering under wet blankets.

One of the world's worst forest fires was in Illinois in 1871, when a wall of flame swept rapidly along the shores of Lake Michigan, destroying over a million acres of forest and killing more than 1,000 people. Survivors describe a whirlwind of flames that rose above the treetops. Some people were killed by breathing in the super-heated air.

Fighting forest fires requires a two-pronged attack. First, specialized crews fly over the blaze in water bombers. Then, once the blaze is under control, regular firefighters attend the scene. Hundreds of extras from the army or civilian populations may be called in as reinforcements.

A helicopter hovers above a forest fire, ready to drop water from its bucket (*above*).

THE AFTERMATH

Firefighters move in to beat out a forest fire (above). These fires can be extremely difficult to deal with because of the speed at which they move and the enormous temperatures that are reached. In Australia, the heat of a bush fire twisted huge steel girders and machinery as if they were toys.

FRUITS AND NUTS

Once fertilization has taken place, the ovule develops into a seed. The ovary around it grows into a protective covering, called the fruit. There are many different forms of fruit – berries, nuts, pods, fleshy fruits, or, in the case of conifers, cones. The fruit protects the seeds and its shape helps them get carried to a suitable place to grow. Fruits and nuts are often tasty and nutritious – they have evolved this way to attract animals, which will eat them and disperse the seeds.

A VARIETY OF FRUITS AND NUTS FROM TREES

Coconut

Grapefruit

Plum

Lemon

Pear

Walnut

Apple

Cob nut

1

2

A bee pollinates an apple blossom and fertilization takes place (1). The flower dies, its job done (2). The ovary and base of the flower develop into a fleshy fruit around the apple seeds, or pits (3).

3

The first foods

Fruits and nuts were among humankind's first foods. Our early ancestors would gather these foods from the trees near them. However, depending on wild trees for food can be risky, so thousands of years ago, people began to cultivate fruit-bearing trees from seeds. These small orchards supplied a more stable source of food than gathering could provide.

Ancient Egyptian orchard

106

Nuts to music

Nuts are large, dry, edible seeds with a strong husk (the fruit) protecting the flesh. This shell is usually discarded after the nut itself has been eaten. But some nutshells can make percussion instruments. On old radio shows, the two halves of a coconut shell were clapped together to make the sound of horse's hooves. You can use them as a rhythm instrument. Smaller nuts, like pine kernels, can be enclosed in a plastic cup to make a shaker, or *maraca*.

Dispersal

Fruits are designed for various methods of dispersal. Trees cannot move, so seeds must be carried away from them, where there will not be as much competition for light and water.

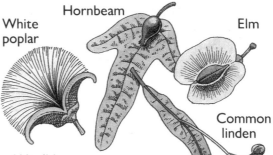

White poplar — Hornbeam — Elm — Common linden

Windblown

Some seeds have light wings that help them to travel. The wind carries them spinning through the air away from the tree. Others have white, downy parachutes that float in the wind.

Carried by animals

Mammals and birds eat the soft fruits, berries, and nuts of trees and drop the seeds to the ground. Some seeds can also pass through animals' digestive systems unharmed.

Cherries

Bursting forth

The seeds of some trees are protected by pods until they ripen and the pods break open to release the seeds. The pods of different tree species vary in shape.

Laburnum

Waterborne

The white flesh of a coconut is actually a large seed. Its shell, covered with coarse fibers, acts as a float and carries the seed across the seas. When it reaches a beach, it can take root and grow.

Coconut

Orange

Fig

Avocado

Horse chestnut

Loquat fruit

Marsupials

Marsupials, or pouched mammals, differ from humans in that they carry their underdeveloped newborns in a pouch outside the mother's stomach. They feed on grass and other plant life, and mostly inhabit grasslands and forests. There are several types of marsupials, such as kangaroos, wombats, opossums, wallabies, and Koala bears.

The Red Kangaroo is the largest of the marsupials. It can grow as large as 6½ feet long and 200 pounds in weight. However, at birth they are only ¾ inch long and 1/30 oz. The baby is born after only five weeks in its mother's womb, and spends the next six months inside her pouch feeding on her milk.

The babies of most mammals grow and develop inside their mother's body until they are fully formed. They get all their nutrients from a sack inside the womb called a placenta. *But female marsupials do not have placentas; their babies come out of the womb at a very early stage and suckle milk constantly until they can look after themselves.*

marsupial mouse

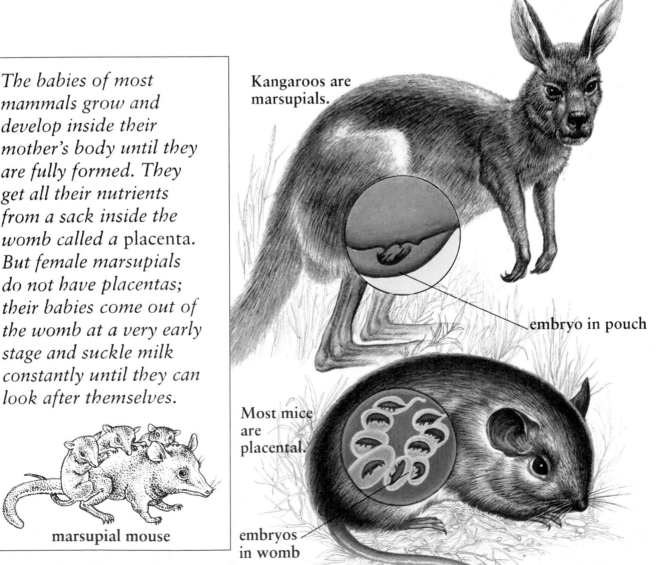

Kangaroos are marsupials.

embryo in pouch

Most mice are placental.

embryos in womb

◁ A mother Gray Kangaroo with her young in her pouch

Yellow-bellied sea snake

Banded sea snake

Beaked Killers

Sea snakes only grow to 8 feet (2.5m), but most are highly poisonous. They pose little threat to humans, because they remain far from the shore. But the beaked sea snake that lives in the muddy shallows of Southeast Asia kills thousands of people each year.

THE EVIL SERPENT

March 23, 1830. The schooner _Eagle_, bound for Charleston, South Carolina, was making good time when the starboard lookout started shouting. Captain Deland raised his telescope and scanned the horizon. Yes, there was something strange out there. He changed course toward what seemed to be an enormous serpent, basking in the sun. Deland ordered a man to shoot at it. The musket ball struck the creature on the back, sending it diving beneath the waves in a huge cloud of spray. It then swam below the ship and struck it several times with its tail before disappearing. What was this strange creature?

Rhinomuraena sea snake

Light vs. Dark

In ancient Egyptian mythology, the greatest god was Re (or Atum), the sun-god creator of the universe. His great enemy was Apophis (right), an evil serpentlike creature. Every night, Re fought Apophis to restore light the next day.

THE REAL SERPENTS?

Many sea serpent tales probably began with sightings of conger eels, or pythons swimming from one island to another. Eels are one of the few truly aggressive sea creatures. Moray eels can give a nasty nip, but this is nothing compared with a bite from a 12-foot (4-m), 220-pound (100-kg) conger eel (below).

Shocking

Some fish can generate large electrical currents within their bodies. The electric eel can produce a stunning 650 volts. Smaller electric fish, such as some species of skates, also use their bodies' electric fields as navigation aids.

JORMUNGARD, the huge serpent of Norse mythology, is coiled around the world, biting its own tail (main picture).

OAR–SOME!

Another source of sea monster mythology is the huge oarfish (right). Its body, flattened like an oar, can grow up to 26 feet (8m) in length. The crest on its head gives it an even weirder appearance.

ANIMALS IN WATER

From seas and oceans, to rivers, lakes and ponds, the waters of the Earth teem with all sorts of animal life. Fish live in water all the time, while animals, such as frogs, are amphibious (specially adapted to living on land and in water), and only spend part of their life-cycle in water. Some of the largest animals in the world, such as the whale, can only live in water, because it supports their massive body. Ocean currents carry sea mammals, fish and microscopic animals, called zooplankton, around the world. Most animals are adapted to either fresh or salt water, but a few, such as eels and salmon, can survive in both.

Water birds
Ducks, geese and swans have webbed feet which help them swim. Rails and coots have long toes to walk over soft mud without sinking in. Long legs allow herons and storks to wade in deep water.

Animals in shells
Shellfish, such as crabs, limpets and mussels, have strong, hard shells to protect their soft bodies. Crabs are scavengers, eating almost anything edible from the seabed or seashore.

Crab

Mussels

Limpets

Insects
Water bugs, such as water boatmen and water beetles, inhabit freshwater ponds, slow-moving streams and still pools.

Eel

Fish
Roach and bream are freshwater fish which live in lakes and rivers all over Europe. Eels can survive in both salt and fresh water.

Bream

Roach

Water boatman

Sea mammals
Dolphins, sea cows and whales, like this humpback whale (left), spend their whole lives in the water. Thick layers of fat, called blubber, help to keep them warm. They come to the surface to breathe air through a blowhole on the top of the head. Other sea mammals include seals, sea lions and walruses.

Dolphins and porpoises have a smooth, sleek, streamlined shape. Water flows past them easily, allowing them to swim faster.

Mermaids

Mermaids have appeared in stories about the sea for hundreds of years. The top half of a mermaid is like a woman, and the bottom half is like a fish. People used to believe that mermaids lured sailors to their deaths with their beauty and enchanted singing.

Breathing in water

All animals need to take in oxygen, which allows them to release energy from their food. There is oxygen dissolved in water which fish absorb by gulping in water and forcing it over tiny, feather-like structures called gills (shown right). Gills are rich in blood vessels, and oxygen is absorbed directly into the blood and carried around the body. Like other animals which breathe oxygen, fish produce carbon dioxide as a waste product. It passes from the blood through the gills and into the water. Gills or gill-like structures, are also found in mollusks (animals in shells), crabs, and water insects, such as mayfly nymphs.

Gill

Otter

Mammals

Otters are specially adapted to living both in and out of water. They have soft underfur which traps air, keeping water out and body heat in, and webbed feet for swimming.

Leeches and medicine

Doctors once believed that too much blood in the body was the cause of some diseases. They put water animals, called leeches, on a patient's body to suck out some of the blood. When a leech feeds, it produces a chemical that stops blood from clotting (thickening). A single leech can rapidly take in three or four times its own weight in blood.

Reptiles

Most reptiles live on land but some, such as sea-turtles, crocodiles, and alligators, spend much of their lives in the water, coming to land mainly to lay eggs. Turtles swim with their paddle-like flippers, while crocodiles and alligators use their powerful, flattened tails for swimming.

Crocodiles and turtles are ancient reptiles which have lived in the world's seas and rivers for thousands of years.

WHAT ARE PLAGUES?

A plague is an invasion by large numbers of animals or insects. The animals often carry disease, and they eat enormous quantities of growing crops and stored grain. This can bring about a severe famine.

Some of the most destructive plagues consist of swarms of locusts. A single swarm may contain up to 50 billion insects.

Plagues of locusts have threatened several African countries in recent years. Rains in 1988 helped to relieve the drought. However, when combined with warmer weather, they provided ideal conditions for the locusts to breed. As a result, swarms of migratory locusts swept across North and Central Africa, destroying the much-needed harvest there.

Locusts

▲ Locusts can strip bare a whole field of maize in less than one hour.
▼ By June 1988, locusts were reported in every African country in a belt, stretching from Cape Verde in the west to the Sudan in the east.

▷ **Locusts fly thousands of miles in search of food. Locust invasions, such as the one in Dakar, Senegal, shown right, have plagued farmers throughout the world since ancient times. Locusts will eat any kind of vegetation, and can consume more than their own body weight in food in just one day.**

◁ ▽ **A locust is a type of adult grasshopper with wings. Its body is about 2 inches (6cm) long. The female locust can produce hundreds of eggs in a single breeding season. As locusts become crowded and restless, they begin to migrate in swarms to other areas. The swarms can be so large, they block out the sunlight.**

Kangaroos

Animal plagues can also involve large mammals such as kangaroos and goats. More than 3 million kangaroos are killed in Australia each year. Australian farmers consider that some of the 50 different kinds of kangaroo are pests. They feed and drink in the same areas as the farmers' sheep and cattle.

Controlling the kangaroo population has proved difficult as they cannot easily be contained by fencing.

TYPES OF DINOSAURS

Dinosaurs are probably the best-known form of prehistoric life. They ruled the Earth from the Late Triassic until the end of the Cretaceous, a total of 165 million years. Although we usually think of dinosaurs as one group (or order) of animal, two distinct types existed. The first were the saurischian, or lizard-hipped dinosaurs. Saurischian dinosaurs included the theropods (meat-eaters) and the giant sauropods (plant-eaters). The second group were the ornithischians, or bird-hipped dinosaurs. Most plant-eating dinosaurs were ornithischians.

The first dinosaurs

In 1842, Sir Richard Owen recognized that some large bones found years before were different from living reptiles and he grouped them together as the "Dinosauria." The first creature to be described was *Megalosaurus*, a large carnivorous dinosaur found in the Jurassic rocks of the Cotswolds in England. Two others were herbivores, and of Cretaceous age. *Hylaeosaurus* was an armored dinosaur.

The Jurassic world

By the Jurassic, dinosaurs ruled the Earth. During the early Jurassic, the most common dinosaurs were the prosauropods, ancestors of the sauropods (reptile feet); small ornithischians, for example, the fabrosaurs; and the carnivorous *Megalosaurus*. By the Middle Jurassic, the giant sauropods like *Cetiosaurus* and *Brachiosaurus* came into their own. Other herbivores included stegosaurs (plated reptiles), and a selection of ornithopods (bird feet) such as the hypsilophodonts. These animals were hunted by *Megalosaurus* and *Ornithomimius*.

Jurassic

The Triassic world

The Triassic world was dominated by many groups of large vertebrates including rhynchosaurs and thecodontians. Dinosaurs evolved from the thecodontians, and first appeared in great numbers during the Late Triassic.

Masrocnemus

Rhynchosaur

Triassic

Dinostars

One of the most successful dinosaur films is Steven Spielberg's *Jurassic Park* (right), based on the book of the same name by Michael Crichton. Jurassic Park is a dinosaur theme park created by a businessman. But things go horribly wrong! The dinosaurs were brought to life for the movie by computer graphics and model animation. It's probably the most realistic dinosaur film ever made.

Cretaceous

We know from fossils that many dinosaurs laid eggs. Some fossil eggs (below) have been found containing babies.

Cretaceous world

At the end of the Cretaceous, the reign of the dinosaurs ended. This may have been caused by a meteorite hitting the Earth. Evidence for this comes from the iridium layer (marked by the white circle below) which is a rare element found at the Cretaceous-Tertiary boundary. Other theories suggest dinosaurs died out due to a change in climate.

Iridium layer

Hot-blooded or not?

Dinosaurs used to be thought of as large, slow, stupid reptiles. But today, even though scientists think they led more active lives, the question of their metabolism (how their bodies produced heat) has still not been decided. Some people think that dinosaurs were warm-blooded, like mammals, generating their own body heat without having to use the sun's rays to warm them up. However, most scientists agree that the large size of their bodies probably meant that a dinosaur stayed warm, even though it could not produce heat internally. This meant they could act in an almost "warm-blooded" manner.

SNOW, ICE, & HAIL

High in the sky, where the air temperature is below the freezing point of water, droplets of water in the clouds turn into ice crystals. More water then freezes on to the ice crystals, which grow bigger. As these crystals fall down through the cloud, they bump into other crystals and may form snowflakes. If the temperature near the ground is below freezing, snow falls from the clouds. But if it is above freezing, the snowflakes melt and fall as rain or half-melted snow, called sleet. Icebergs are huge lumps of ice that break off the polar ice caps.

Icy hazards

An avalanche can bury a village in seconds and smash trees as if they were matchsticks. It can happen when fresh snow falls on top of an icy layer on slopes. Avalanches can be triggered by a rise in temperature, a strong wind or even a loud noise. Icebergs are also a hazard. The passenger liner, Titanic, sank in April 1912 after hitting an iceberg. Lumps of ice that fall off icebergs are known as bergy bits, and even smaller lumps are called growlers.

Jumping hailstones

Hailstones are hard lumps of ice formed in cumulonimbus clouds when crystals of ice are thrown up and down by strong air currents. Ice builds up in layers around the ice crystals. Clear layers build up in the lower part of the cloud where it is warmer and the water freezes slowly; frosty ice layers form when the crystal is higher up in the cloud. By counting the layers, you can tell how many times a hailstone was tossed up and down inside a cloud.

This hailstone was tossed up and down five times in a cloud

Tracks in snow

Animal footprints in fresh snow provide clues to the variety of wildlife in an area. They show something of how the animals moved and what they were doing before you arrived on the scene. Can you guess which animals made these tracks? The answers are at the bottom of the page. You may find similar tracks in mud.

A   B

C. Domestic cat D. Mouse

Each snowflake is different although they all have six sides. The shape and size of snowflakes depends on the height and temperature at which they are formed and the amount of moisture in the cloud. In cold air, they are needle or rod-shaped; in warmer air, they are star- or plate-shaped.

Frost forms when the temperature drops below 32°F

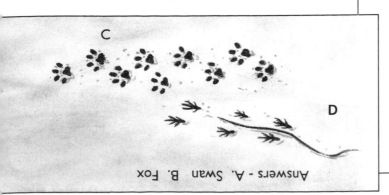

C

D

Answers - A. Swan B. Fox

Jack Frost

The legendary Jack Frost is an elf-like figure who is supposed to leave his icy fingermarks on windowpanes. Beautiful patterns sometimes form on windows when water vapor turns directly to ice as it touches the freezing glass. The legend of Jack Frost probably comes from Norse Mythology, where Kari, god of the winds, had a son called Jokul (meaning icicle), or Frosti (meaning frost).

Jack Frost

The Ice Man

In September 1991, hikers in the Alps came across the body of a man who turned out to be over 5,000 years old. He was preserved by being sealed in an airtight pocket beneath the ice of a glacier and the intense cold stopped his body decaying in the usual way. He was still wearing a boot stuffed with grass and his brain and internal organs were still intact. Bodies caught in glaciers are usually crushed and torn by the ice, so the fact that this body was preserved was pure chance. Scientists think the ice man froze to death after falling asleep. He may have been a mountain shepherd who had lost his weapons and was collecting material to make new ones.

The Ice Man

FISH COURTSHIP

Animals use courtship behavior to make sure that they are pairing up with a mate of the same species, and one who is fit and healthy. In this way, the mating is likely to produce healthy offspring. Fish courtship is not usually so spectacular as it is in many birds and mammals. Most fish come together only fleetingly to mate, and then go their own way again. However, some pond and coral reef fish use visual displays and courtship behavior in the brightly lit waters of their habitats.

Courting and caring

In most species of fish, the female lays her eggs (roe), the male adds his milky sperm (milt) to fertilize them, and then the eggs are left on their own. However, some fish have complex courtships, and care for their babies. The male stickleback (below) entices a female to his nest by showing off his bright breeding colors. He also cares for his young as they develop in the nest. So does the male seahorse, in a "pocket" on his belly.

Father gives birth

The seahorse is a strangely-shaped fish related to the stickleback. After the female lays her eggs, the male gathers them into the brood pouch on his front. The babies develop in this protected place. A few weeks later their father "gives birth" through the small opening of the pouch.

The mating dance

In spring, the male stickleback's underside goes bright red and his eyes turn bright blue. He builds a nest of plant debris on the bottom. Then he swims around a female in a zig-zag courting dance, attracting her with his bright colors. He encourages her to the nest. She lays her eggs and he adds his sperm – the process known as spawning.

Prized eggs

Sturgeons are massive fish ten to thirteen feet long, with large back scales and pointed snouts. The salted, unlaid eggs of the female sturgeon form the delicacy called caviar. At one time sturgeons were common, and even poor people ate caviar. But centuries of overfishing have made sturgeons very rare, and caviar very expensive.

Bred for beauty

For centuries, people have selected and bred together certain specimens of fish. This has been done to enhance their natural shapes and colors, or in the hope of producing new features such as frilly fins or goggle eyes. Koi and other carp have been bred in China and Japan for over 4,000 years. The goldfish was produced by selective breeding about 1,600 years ago.

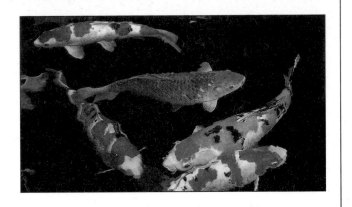

Places for protection

Some fish lay their eggs in a protected place, such as under a rock or among weeds, where they are less likely to be noticed and eaten by other fish. Many cichlids, freshwater fish from warm climates, keep their eggs in their mouths! Usually the female does this, a process known as mouth-brooding. Other fish, like sharks and rays, lay eggs with tough, leathery cases (below) that protect the developing young inside.

Baby cichlids swim in a cloud around the mother's head. But they are ready to dash back into her mouth if danger threatens.

Life cycle of the salmon

Salmon spawn (lay eggs and sperm) in the shallow waters of small inland streams. The eggs hatch and the young salmon spend several years in the river, before migrating to sea where they become mature. To breed, the adults battle from the sea and make their way upriver. Surveys on tagged fish show that each salmon returns to the very stream where it hatched. It probably finds its way by its chemosenses.

Hanger-on

In the vast, inky depths of the sea, it is difficult to find a suitable partner. So when a male deep-sea anglerfish meets a female, he joins himself to her body. He becomes more and more firmly attached until his body is fused to hers. The female has a male at hand ready to fertilize her eggs. But she also has one or several hangers-on, or "parasites," who she carries everywhere, and who she has to supply with food.

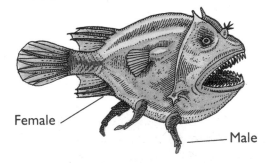

Female

Male

WHAT IF A TIGER HAD NO TEETH?

Carnassial teeth

It would soon go hungry and starve. The tiger uses its claws to catch and scratch prey. But it needs its teeth to deliver the deadly bites, and to slice the meat off the bones for eating. The tiger has two main kinds of teeth for these jobs. The long, sharp canines or "fangs" are at the front of the mouth. They stab, wound, and skin the victim, making it bleed, suffocate, and die.

The large, ridge-edged carnassial teeth at the back of the mouth come together like the blades of scissors when the tiger closes its jaws. These very strong teeth carve off and slice up the meat, and can even crunch gristle (cartilage) and soft bones.

Canine teeth

Purr-fect claws

A cat's claws are vital for its survival in the wild. With these incredibly sharp weapons, the hunter can slash, stab, and pin prey that will become its food. However, these deadly claws need to be kept razor sharp for the next kill. To ensure this, most cats can withdraw, or retract, their claws into sheaths in the toes.

This allows the cat to run, walk, and jump without scraping its sharp talons along the ground. It keeps them sharp, unbroken, and clean. It keeps them from getting blunt or getting tangled in twigs, grass, bark, and other things. When the cat needs its claws to climb a tree or to slash and pin its prey, it makes them stick out of the toes.

Claws indoors

The cat's claw is equivalent to your fingernail or toenail. But the claw can swing or pivot on its toe bone. A muscle in the lower leg pulls on a long, stringlike tendon that is attached to the bone and claw. This pulls the sharp claw out of its protective sheath.

Bone

Tendon

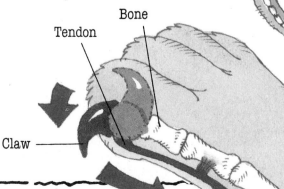

Claw

Plant-eating carnivore

When the giant panda of China was first discovered, it posed a problem to scientists. It has the sharp, fanglike teeth of a carnivore (meat-eater), and is indeed a close relative of the meat-eating raccoon. However, its diet consists almost solely of bamboo shoots. Even though it can eat meat, the panda chooses the young shoots of this type of grass. Unfortunately, bamboo is very low in nutritional value. As a result, it must spend nearly all of its time sitting around, lazily eating in order to consume enough to survive.

Highly-sprung hunter

The fastest hunter on land owes its speed to its flexible backbone. Without this powerful spring running along its spine, the cheetah would not be able to catch and kill the nimble prey that it hunts, such as gazelle and springbok.

As this big cat sprints, the spine flexes, stretching the body out, and allowing the legs to cover even more distance with each stride. This makes the cheetah the world's fastest runner, at over 60 mph (100 km/h).

As the cheetah's legs come together, the spine bends up in the middle.

As the cheetah extends its legs, the spine flattens and arches backward.

As a result the legs can stretch further apart, letting the cheetah run faster.

WHAT ARE MAMMALS?

Mammals are the most successful animals with backbones on Earth today. There are about 4,500 species, and they live in all habitats, from the coldest to the hottest, on land, in the sea, and in the air. Each one looks different, but in certain ways they are all alike. Mammals have large brains and keen senses. They communicate by sounds, smells, and visual means. They are warm-blooded, have an efficient circulation system and they care for their young. Human beings can even change their environment.

Mother's Milk

One of the reasons for the success of mammals is the care that they give to their young. Mothers provide instant food until the babies are big enough to feed themselves. This food, a liquid secretion called *milk*, contains nutrients and immunity to some diseases. It is made by mammary glands under the mother's skin, and the baby sucks it from nipples during nursing.

First Mammals

The last 65 million years, since the dinosaurs died out, has been the "Age of Mammals." But the first mammals appeared long before this, about 200 million years ago. They evolved from a group of mammal-like reptiles that were successful even before the reign of the dinosaurs. *Megazostrodon* and *Purgatorius* were among the first true mammals. These tiny animals hid in trees and undergrowth, hunting insects at night.

Taeniolabis (An early plant eater)

Purgatorius

Megazostrodon

Warm Blood

Mammals can live in any climate because they are warm-blooded, or *endothermic*. This means they can keep their bodies at the same temperature no matter how cold or hot the weather is. Endotherms generate heat by chemical reactions that go on inside the body tissues. They keep this heat in with layers of insulating fat and fur. If they get too hot, most mammals can produce sweat. Sweat is a liquid secreted onto the skin surface which evaporates and cools the body.

124

Food, Clothes, and Shelter

When people migrated from the warmth of Africa, where they first evolved, to colder northern latitudes, they began to use the skins of other mammals to keep themselves warm. In the far north, where there were no caves and no trees to build huts, they used colossal mammoth bones and tusks for the framework of shelters. This may have led to the first man-made extinctions, about 10,000 years ago, when the mammoths died out.

Aesop's Fables

Aesop was a Greek storyteller who lived in the 6th century B.C. He used animal stories to show people how to deal with life's little problems, and to teach right from wrong. One story (below) tells of a race between a slow tortoise (a reptile) and a swift hare (a mammal). The hare is so far ahead, and so confident of victory, he takes a nap. The tortoise plods

along steadily, passing the hare, who wakes up to see his opponent crossing the finishing line. The tale teaches that persistence can be more important than speed.

Vertebrates

Mammals belong to the group of animals known as *vertebrates*. They all have backbones as part of their internal skeletons. Skeletons provide support and protection for internal organs and enable movement. A gorilla's skeleton (left) is similar to that of an orang-utan (above).

Adaptable Mammals

After the demise of the dinosaurs, mammals soon adapted to fill every habitat. Some mammals are perfectly adapted to a particular habitat. Dolphins are so well adjusted to life in the water they can no longer live on land. Others survive by being adaptable. The wolf lives by its wits, eating almost anything it can find, and taking advantage of any situation.

WHAT IF THE CONTINENTS DIDN'T MOVE?

The land under your feet may seem solid and still. But each main landmass, or continent, is drifting very slowly across the face of the Earth, by less than 2 inches (5 cm) each year. The Earth's outer "skin," or crust, is made up of 12 giant, curved plates, like a vast, ball-shaped puzzle. They are called *lithospheric (curved-rock) plates*. As the plates rub against each other, their edges crack or get pushed deeper. Some plates enlarge, while others shrink. This has been going on since the Earth began, 4.5 billion years ago.

We would see some strange animal meetings!

The plates under the ocean are thinner. Molten rock from deep below becomes solid, adds to the plate, pushing it sideways.

An oceanic plate pushes into a continental plate. The oceanic plate is forced down and an ocean trench forms.

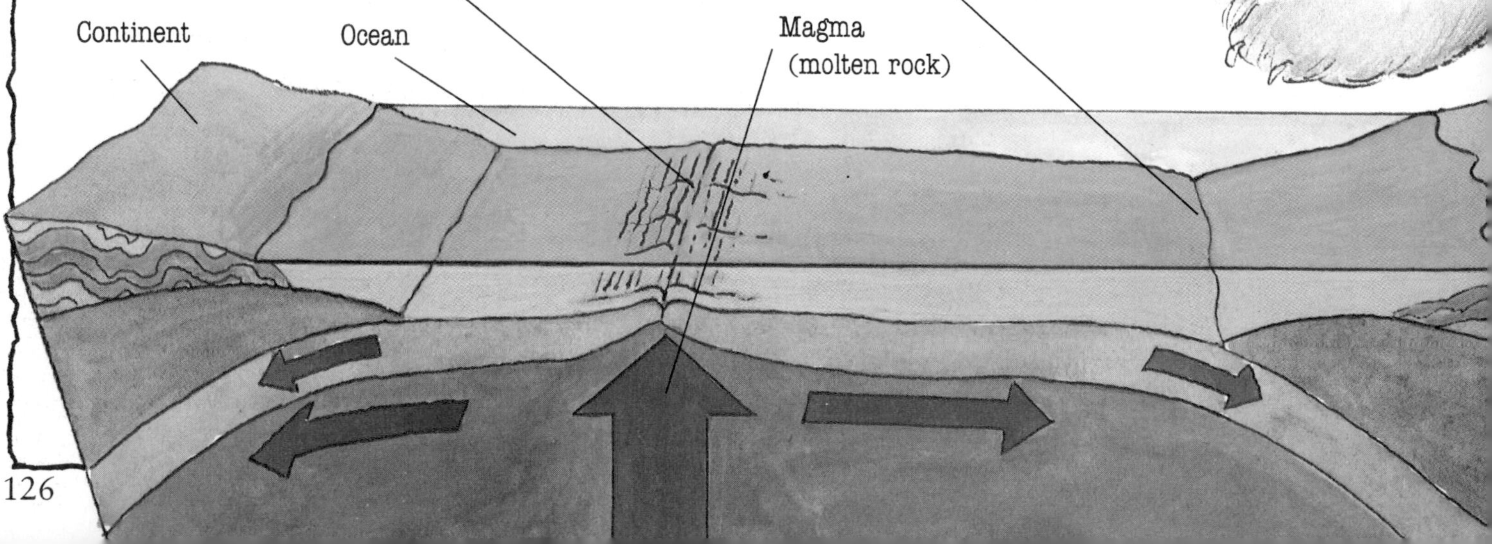

Continent   Ocean

Magma (molten rock)

Rock steady

Without continental drift, there could be no metamorphic rocks, like marble. These form when other rocks are squeezed incredibly hard in the roots of new mountains. Igneous rocks, like granite, form when melted rock, such as the lava from volcanoes, cools and solidifies. Sedimentary rocks, such as chalk, form when tiny particles settle in a lake or sea, and get pressed and cemented together.

Pangaea

Metamorphic rock

Igneous rock

Sedimentary rock

Mapping out the world

About 250 million years ago all the continents were joined into one vast land mass, the super-continent of Pangaea. The continuous ocean around it was the Tethys Sea. If continental drift had stopped, the map would still look like this. A journey from North America to Europe, or South America to Africa, could be by car!

The layers of rock in the continental plate are crumpled by movements. This creates huge folds – mountains.

Highs and lows!

The world would be much flatter and less exciting without continental drift. The deepest part of the oceans, the Marianas Trench in the Pacific, and the highest mountain, Mount Everest in the Himalayas, wouldn't exist.

Fold mountains

SEASHORE LIFE

The seashore is one of the harshest surroundings for living things. Twice a day these creatures are covered by water, then dry out as the tide goes out. They are exposed to heat, cold, and buffeting waves. Conditions keep changing. But each tide brings in a new supply of food in the form of microscopic sea creatures. In spite of the difficulties, many sea animals live on shores. Seaweeds grow among rocks where the water is shallow enough for them to get the light they need. There is a huge number of kinds, but by observation and taking notes you will find you soon get to know the main ones. The seashore is one of the places that is most fun for a naturalist. There is always something to see, and you are never sure what will be in the next pool.

SHORE ZONES
If you map seaweed types on a rocky shore you will find they live at different levels on the beach. The same is true for many of the animals.

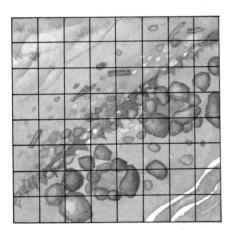

Laver

Limpets

Barnacles

Small periwinkles

Bladder wrack

Starfish

Lobster

Sea wrack

Shore crab

Whelks

SEARCHING THE BEACH

To discover which animals live along a shore, especially at the lower levels, follow the tide out down the beach. Many animals will have hidden in crevices and beneath rock ledges, others may be lurking in rocky tide pools, so you should be able to get close enough to study them.

Gulls are successful scavengers. You will see them swoop down to catch crabs or to gobble up any small fish that may have become tangled in seaweed and stranded by the tide.

Black headed gull

Sea bindweed

Hermit crab

Common dog whelk

VARYING TIDES
The height of the tides varies throughout a month, but parts of the shore are only wetted by the highest spring tides. Some sea creatures can only survive where they are just splashed by spray.

Splash zone

SPRING TIDE
HIGH TIDE
LOW TIDE

LARGER SPECIES

Seals swim near the shore and may climb out to rest if they don't see you. Dolphins and porpoises sometimes play close by the shore. Search the strandline for the remains of these and other dead animals washed up on the beach after storms.

MAKING TRACKS
Seals are graceful swimmers, but are clumsy on land. If they cross sand they may leave tracks like these.

Gray seal and tracks

Bottle-nosed dolphin

Pilot whale

Loggerhead turtle

CROCODILES AND ALLIGATORS

The 22 species of crocodilians are all lurking predators, which also scavenge meat from any dead carcass left by another hunter. They live in tropical regions, in or near water, and spend much of the day basking in the sun to keep warm. The powerful tail and rear limbs are used to propel the animal through the water. The caimans of South America have the shortest, broadest snouts and eat the most varied diet, including frogs, snakes, lizards, birds, and mammals. The gavial of the Indian region has a long, narrow snout and eats mainly fish.

Caiman

Alligator

Crocodile

Gavial

Adapted for water
The alligator is well suited for a watery life. Its broad tail gives powerful swimming propulsion (opposite) and it can hold its breath for minutes at a time.

Strong rear limbs with webbed feet

Front limbs are smaller. Front feet are not webbed.

Crocodilians worldwide
The map shows the distribution of some of the main species of crocodilians. The two main groups are the crocodiles, with 14 species, and alligators, with 7 species, which includes the caimans. The Estuarine crocodile is the only one that lives in salt water.

Key
- Common caiman
- American alligator
- American crocodile
- Nile crocodile
- Estuarine crocodile
- Gavial

The swishing tail

The tail is arched from side to side by powerful muscles running down the animal's body. The main part of the body is relatively stiff and takes little part in swimming.

With a crocodile's help

The crocodile features in many stories. In *The Just So Stories* by Rudyard Kipling (1902) a crocodile seizes a young elephant by its nose, which is "no bigger than a boot." The elephant tries to get away, and its nose stretches – which is how, supposedly, the elephant got its trunk!

From rare to common

American alligators live in the southeastern United States. They were hunted so much for their skins and because they threatened people and livestock, that they became in danger of extinction (dying out completely). Wildlife laws were introduced in 1969 to protect them. In 1987 the species was declared to be out of danger of extinction. Today they are more common and a few are hunted (below).

Crocodile swimming

The main swimming power for crocodilians comes from the deep tail, which swishes from side to side like a fish's tail. This pushes the animal forward. The front legs are usually held up against the underside of the body, for better streamlining. The rear legs can be used for steering, and for paddling at slow speeds. By thrusting its rear feet forward and up, with its webbed toes spread, a crocodile can suddenly stop moving forward and sink down under the water.

Crocodile songs

Crocodilians feature in various plays and also in popular songs. These include *See You Later Alligator* (1956), the early rock'n'roll jive-talking hit by Bill Haley and the Comets, and *Crocodile Rock* (1973) by Elton John.

Bill Haley

MAKING A POND ENVIRONMENT

If you have a yard you can construct a real pond, but failing this, a coldwater aquarium can be stocked with plants and animals to make a "natural" habitat. One secret of success is to make sure that the animals have enough oxygen. Choose an aquarium with a big surface, not one that is tall and narrow. Do not overcrowd it, and above all do not put in fierce hunters such as diving beetles and dragonfly larvae that will eat other insects and small fish.

FISH
Goldfish make good pond fish, as they can survive in stagnant water. Sticklebacks are found in all kinds of water. Minnows can live in ponds, but prefer clear, moving water.

Common goldfish

Minnow

Stickleback

Ornamental goldfish

Canadian pond weed

Golden orfe

Arrowhead

PLANTS
Canadian pond weed is useful in pond environments because it puts oxygen into the water. Plants, such as those on the left, give growing and small animals somewhere to hide.

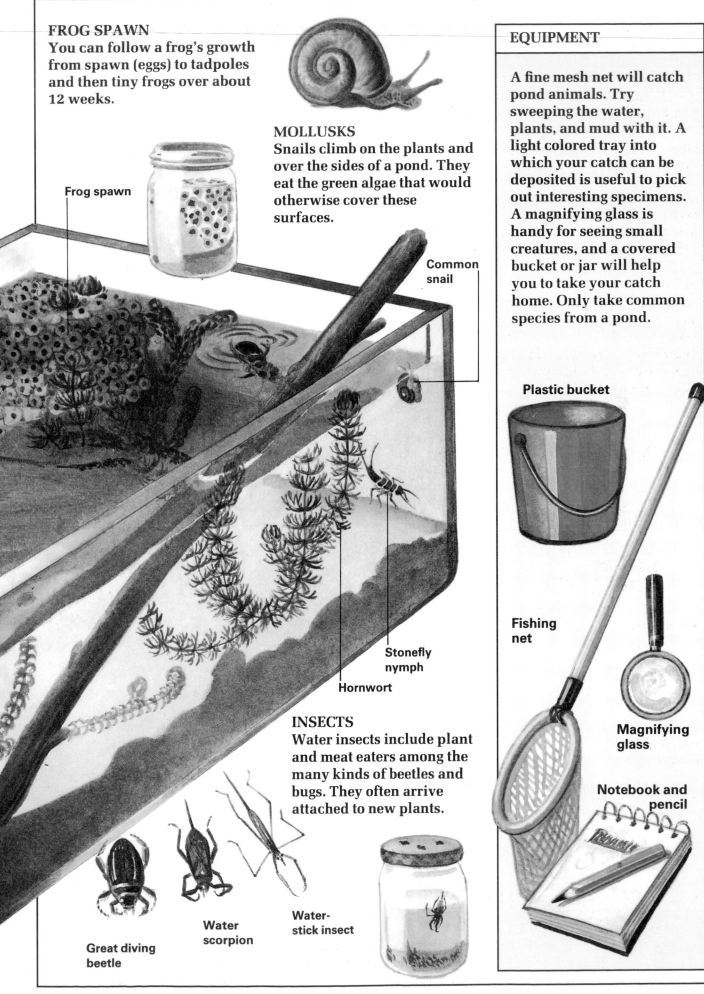

FROG SPAWN
You can follow a frog's growth from spawn (eggs) to tadpoles and then tiny frogs over about 12 weeks.

Frog spawn

MOLLUSKS
Snails climb on the plants and over the sides of a pond. They eat the green algae that would otherwise cover these surfaces.

Common snail

Stonefly nymph

Hornwort

INSECTS
Water insects include plant and meat eaters among the many kinds of beetles and bugs. They often arrive attached to new plants.

Great diving beetle

Water scorpion

Water-stick insect

EQUIPMENT
A fine mesh net will catch pond animals. Try sweeping the water, plants, and mud with it. A light colored tray into which your catch can be deposited is useful to pick out interesting specimens. A magnifying glass is handy for seeing small creatures, and a covered bucket or jar will help you to take your catch home. Only take common species from a pond.

Plastic bucket

Fishing net

Magnifying glass

Notebook and pencil

133

OSTRICH

T HE BIGGEST BIRDS ARE THE OSTRICH from Africa, the emu from Australia, and the rhea from South America. They are too heavy to fly. But these flightless birds, called ratites (pronounced ray-teetz), are suited to life walking and running on the ground.

NECK
The neck is very long. And so, too, are the gullet (esophagus), which carries food down to the digestive system, and the windpipe (trachea), which takes air into the lungs.

WINDPIPE (TRACHEA)

LUNGS

HEART

RIPENING EGGS

FALLOPIAN TUBE

GIZZARD
(grinds up food)

CLAWS
Made of keratin, they are designed to be strong for self-defense, and for scratching around to find food.

BONE
(cutaway to show structure)

An ostrich doesn't really need to fly. It can find food and defend itself very well. On its two long, strong legs, it runs faster than most four-legged animals. It can kick out with its big clawed feet. And peck very hard, too. Ouch!

WINGS
The wings may not be used for flight, but they are still useful. They wave about to impress a breeding partner, flap fiercely at enemies, and shade babies from the sun.

EGG

TAIL
Unlike reptiles and mammals, a bird does not have a backbone in its tail. The tail is made of feathers.

LEG MUSCLES
The muscles around the hip (pelvic bone) and thigh bone (femur) are huge, in order to move the long legs back and forth for running at over 31 miles per hour.

ANATOMY AT WORK
BIGGEST AND SMALLEST
The mother ostrich produces about a dozen of the biggest eggs in the bird group. Yet they are also the smallest eggs in the bird group – in relation to the mother's size. Each one weighs the same as about 25 ordinary chicken's eggs.

PENGUIN

PENGUINS ARE DESIGNED FOR LIFE in cold seas. Their flipper-shaped wings and webbed feet are ideal for swimming. And they are never troubled by polar bears because penguins live in the South Atlantic Ocean and Antarctica, while polar bears live at the other end of the world, in the Arctic north.

COLD FEET
The feet and flippers are designed to be cold. As blood from the warm central body goes into them, it flows next to cooler blood coming back, and is cooled. This reduces heat loss from feet and flippers into the sea, while the returning blood is warmed.

DOWN, DROWN
Like any bird, a penguin needs to breathe fresh air regularly into its lungs. If it is kept underwater for more than a few minutes, it drowns.

ARTERIES
(red)

VEINS
(purple)

AIR SACS

FLAPSTROKE, NOT BACKSTROKE
Penguins can fly – not in the air, but through water. They flap their flipperlike wings up and down, just like any other flying bird, and speed along faster than any human swimmer. However, they cannot do the backstroke.

BONES

MUSCLES

FAT IS FINE
The penguin's stout body has a thick layer of the fatty substance, blubber, just beneath the skin. This helps to keep the cold out. It also makes the body's outline smoother and more streamlined, for swimming.

WINDPIPE
(TRACHEA)

SNAPPER
The strong, stout, sharp-edged beak is ideal for snapping and catching prey such as slippery fish and squid, and hard-cased shellfish.

SALT GLANDS
(for ridding the
blood of excess salt)

ANATOMY AT WORK
STOMACH
After the mouth, gullet, and crop, the next part of a bird's gut is the gizzard, or stomach. This has very thick, muscular walls. Birds cannot chew, so it's the gizzard's job to grind up food.

WHAT IF THE EARTH STOOD STILL?

If it were daytime, the first thing you might notice was that the Sun stopped moving across the sky. You'd wait for evening – but it would never come. It'd be daylight forever! The Earth spins around like a gigantic top on an imaginary line called its axis, that goes through the North and South Poles. It makes one complete turn every 24 hours, giving us the cycle of day and night. As your area of the surface turns, the Sun appears to move across the sky in daytime, and the stars and Moon move across at nighttime.

Direction of Earth's spin

Axis of spin

A still Earth would heat up unbearably on the daytime side.

Daytime on the side facing the Sun

On the shady side, it would be dark, cold, and soon freeze over.

A hard day's night!

If we had endless daytime, the Sun would shine without a break and you might get sunburned. You would also have to go to sleep in bright daylight. People on the other side of the Earth would be in constant cold and darkness. They would become pale and sick.

No more seasons in the Sun?

Besides spinning like a top, the Earth also goes around the Sun in a long, curved path called its *orbit*. One orbit takes one year. The Earth's spinning axis is tilted, so some parts of its surface are closer to the Sun during certain times in the orbit. On these closer parts it is warmer – and summer. If the Earth stopped orbiting and stood still, the seasons would cease, too. It would be endless summer in some areas, and everlasting winter in others!

Spring in north

Sun

Summer in south

Summer in north and winter in south

Fall in north

Winter in north

Nighttime on the side away from the Sun

What would happen to clocks and calendars?

Clocks would keep ticking, and we might continue to use them to tell time. But this would be less useful. We could no longer say things like "It gets dark at 8 o'clock." The calendar would be less useful, too. Without seasons, every month would have the same weather and you would soon get very bored!

How might animals react?

They'd get very confused! Their internal "body clocks" need the pattern of night and day to stay accurate. With no day or night, they wouldn't know when to eat or sleep. With no seasons, they wouldn't know if they should begin a winter's sleep (hibernation) or set off for a long fall or spring journey (migration).

The best place to live

A still Earth would have a very narrow strip on each side, one in constant dawn, and the other in continuous dusk. These areas would not get too bright and hot or too dark and cold. They'd be the best places to live.

Spiders

Spiders are arachnids a large group of arthropods, or animals with segmented bodies and jointed appendages, that live on land. Arachnids, like all arthropods, have an external skeleton. Spiders have eight legs, several eyes (which see very little), and they can produce silk from glands in their abdomen. Spiders use this silk in many ways, but mainly to trap their prey – insects and other small invertebrates.

Spiders also use camouflage to catch their prey. The dull colors of many garden spiders, and their stillness, allow them to trap unwary victims. The *Myrmecium* spider even looks so much like the ants on which it feeds, that it can live in the nest.

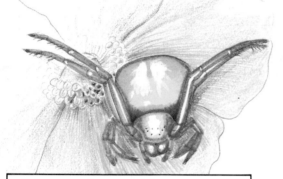

Crab spiders are adapted to the flowers they live on.

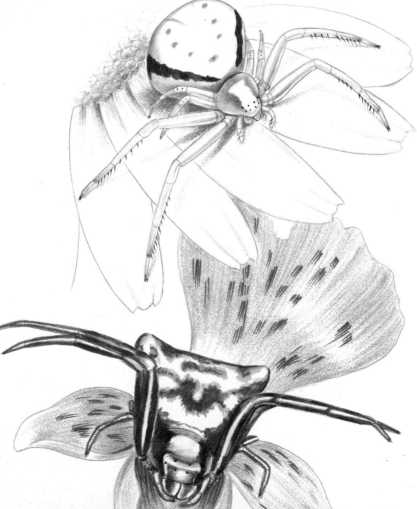

Myrmecium spiders wave their front pair of legs about to look like an insect's antennae. They fool their prey and so can get close enough to attack them.

Ant-mimic spider

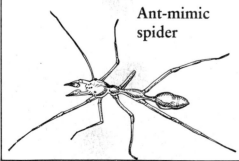

HOW A TREE GROWS

Each year a tree grows thicker, taller, and in some cases, bushier. Its girth increases as a new layer of wood is added to its trunk. This makes the trunk stronger so that it can support the weight of new branches. These grow longer as cells at the branch tips multiply. The tree's roots spread further underground to anchor the tree firmly. The tree also grows new leaves.

Cambium
The cambium produces a new ring of sapwood each year. It makes the trunk and branches thicker and stronger.

Sapwood
Sapwood is made mainly of living cells. It contains tiny tubes that carry water and sap around the tree.

SCOTS PINE

Heartwood
Heartwood is the hard, darker colored dead wood in the middle of the trunk. It supports the tree.

A tree's main areas of growth are at the tips of its branches, around its trunk, and at its root tips. Deciduous trees grow new leaves every year. Evergreen trees may replace their leaves or needles gradually every two or three years.

Tree records
The tallest tree species on Earth is the redwood of California. It has been known

Acacia for a redwood to grow to 370 feet (113 m) tall. The fastest growing tree is the acacia tree of Malaysia, which can grow 36 feet (11 m) in three months. A bristlecone pine in California is the oldest tree — 4,600 years old.

Redwood

1939
On September 3, World War II breaks out after Hitler's Germany invades Poland.

1969
American astronaut Neil Armstrong becomes the first man to step on the moon.

1885
Two German inventors, Daimler and Benz, pioneer the automobile.

1990
What important events happened during this year?

Annual growth rings

Each year, the layer of cambium inside the tree's trunk produces a ring of new wood. This pushes the cambium outward and makes the trunk thicker. These annual rings can be counted to find out how old a tree is. They are also a record of past weather conditions. Wide rings grow in years with plenty of rain. In dry years, the rings are narrow and close together.

There are no annual rings inside a palm tree trunk. Palm trunks contain a mass of unorganized fibers. They do not contain cambium to make new wood, so the trunk never gets wider, only taller.

Rays
Rays carry food and water sideways through the sapwood.

Making a bonsai tree

Bonsais are dwarf trees that are planted in Japanese and Chinese ornamental gardens. Although real bonsais are skillfully sculpted, you can use this shortcut to make your own. You will need to get a dwarf conifer, a shallow tray, compost, scissors, wire, and clippers. Trim the roots of the tree. Then wind wire around the roots to restrict root growth. Plant the tree in the tray and trim the branches to the shape you want. Ensure the tree gets water and light.

3 Snip out branches

2 Bind the root ball with wire

1 Trim the roots

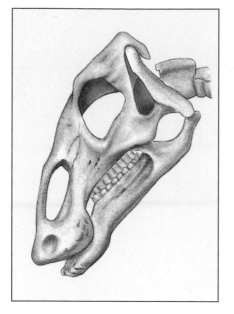

DINOSAURS

Dinosaurs, the word means "terrible lizards," were reptiles which became extinct about 65 million years ago. They lived on the earth for over 140 million years, but the last ones suddenly died out. This was possibly due to a rapid cooling of the planet's climate. Before that time most of the earth was warm and damp so that even in the Arctic Circle there were tropical plants and dinosaurs that ate them. Dinosaurs vanished from the earth millions of years before people evolved. We have to reconstruct what they might have looked like from their fossils. Today the animals that are related most closely to them are crocodiles and birds. Up to now scientists have discovered many hundreds of species of dinosaur.

The Protoceratops, when fully grown to six feet in length, had horns. The discovery of complete nests of fossil eggs (below) told scientists how dinosaurs looked after their young. The baby Protoceratops was about one foot long. The size of dinosaurs varied a lot.

The Brachiosaurus, for example, was 75 feet long and weighed 80 tons. The Cynognathus, from which the tooth (below right) came, was only five feet long. This reptile lived 200 million years ago.

Eggs

Cynognathus

Not all creatures that lived during the "Age of the Dinosaurs" were dinosaurs. Dinosaurs lived on the land. In the air were flying reptiles called pterosaurs, and in the sea were various types of swimming reptiles including plesiosaurs and ichthyosaurs.

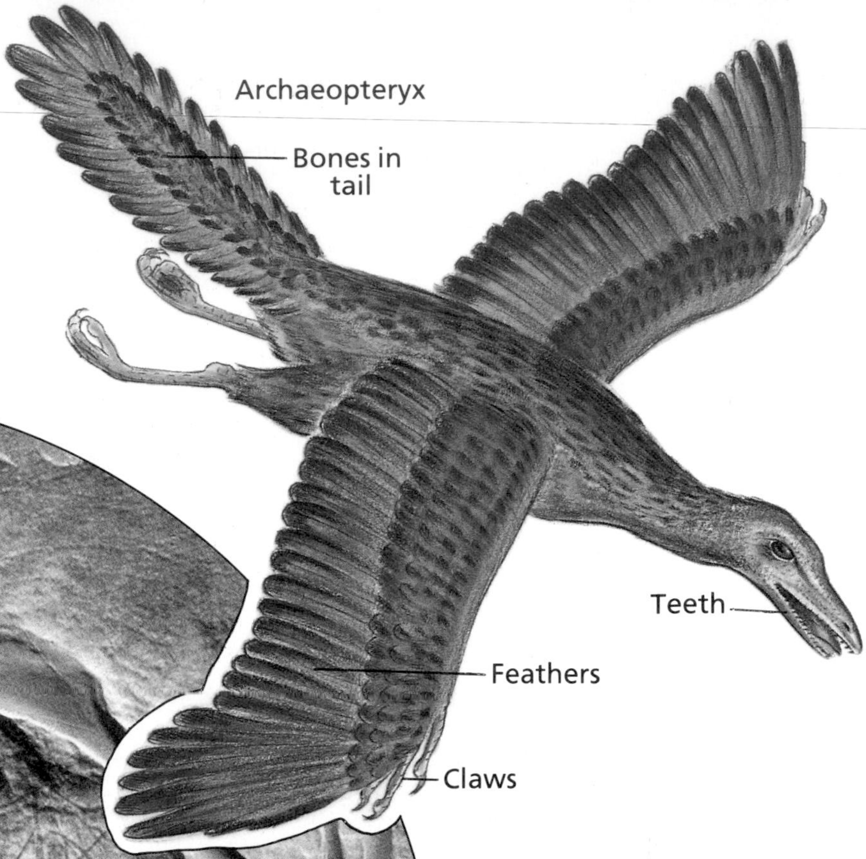

Archaeopteryx

Bones in tail

Teeth

Feathers

Claws

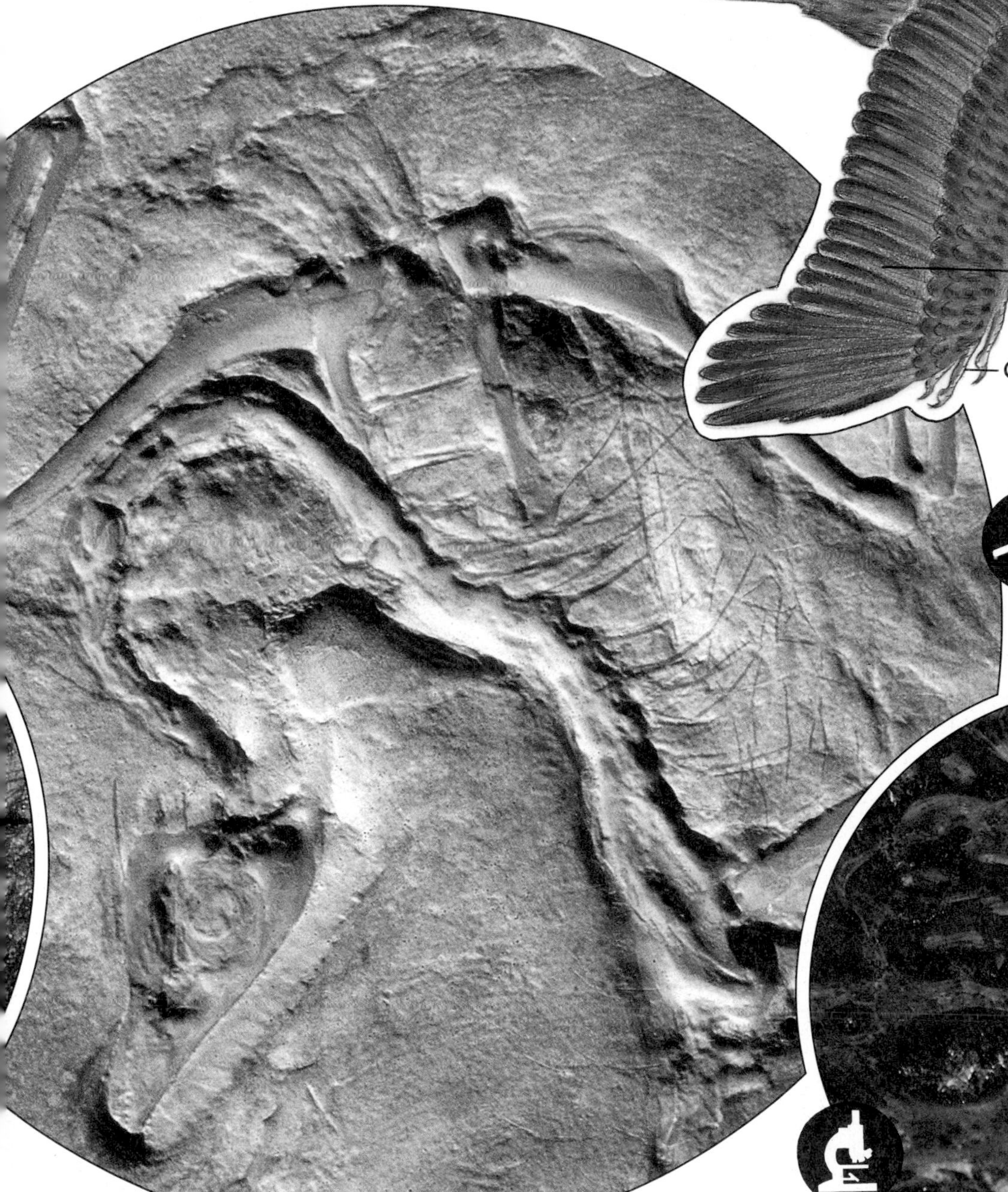

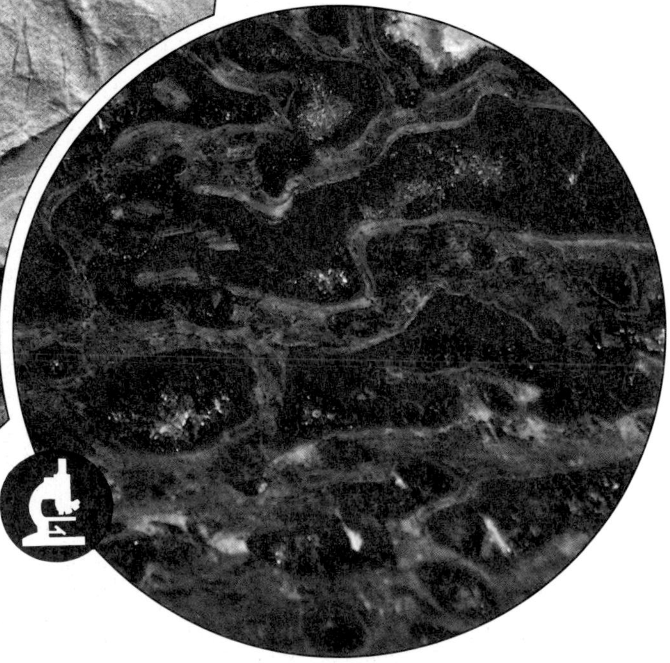

Some people claim that Archaeopteryx, see illustration top right and fossil above, is the missing link between extinct dinosaurs and the birds which we all know today. It was about the same size as a modern crow and ate insects and small reptiles. These strange flying animals had feathers, jaws with sharp teeth, wing claws for climbing trees, and a long bony tail.

Sometimes geologists, investigating rock layers, come across a cluster of fossilized bones. Under a microscope (see above) these can appear to be very beautiful. Paleontologists, scientists who specialize in fossils, will often have to study these finds in detail.

HOOFED ANIMALS

Ungulates walk on the tips of their toes which are protected by hard hooves. Hooves are made from keratin, the same horny material as claws and nails. Solid hooves are an adaptation for running away from predators. Ungulates are divided into three groups: the elephants and their relatives (such as hyraxes); the perissodactyls or odd-toed ungulates, such as horses and zebras; and the artiodactyls or even-toed ungulates, such as cattle.

Odds and Evens

The skeletons of ungulate feet show how they walk on the tips of their toes. Originally all mammals had five digits or toes. But as ungulates evolved they lost toes to improve their speed. Some ungulates, like elephants, still have five toes. Pig trotters have two large hooves and two small hooves which do not touch the ground. Rhinos (upper left) walk on three toes, deer have four (lower left) but walk upon two, and horses have only one.

Diseases

Foot-and-mouth disease affects animals with cloven (split) hooves, such as cattle and sheep. It spreads rapidly through the herds and can bankrupt farmers. Some animal diseases spread to humans. Sleeping sickness is transferred from cattle to humans via the blood-sucking tsetse fly (below).

Mythical Horses

In Ancient Greek mythology, the winged Pegasus flew up to heaven and was tamed by the goddess Athena with a magical golden bridle. The Unicorn is a white horse with a spiral horn growing from its forehead. It is said that whoever drinks from its horn is protected from poisoning.

Migration

Many animals make seasonal migrations to new habitats, to find better living conditions. Huge herds of wildebeest walk hundreds of miles across the African plains in search of grass and water. The urge to move is so strong they will tackle any obstacle. Many die on the way, drowning in rivers, falling down gorges, or caught by predators.

Ungulate Relatives

Camels (left) and llamas are even-toed ungulates. But they do not walk on the tips of their toes like other cloven-hoofed animals. The weight is carried by soft pads behind their hooves. Camels are ideally suited for desert life. Their wide feet do not sink in the sand, their humps store food for long-distance travel, and their stomachs can hold 22 gallons of water. Rhinos are primitive relatives of horses. They have stumpy feet with three hoofed toes, and thick, hairless skin folded into armorlike plates.

Horsemanship

Man's first association with horses was to hunt them for meat. Horses were domesticated in Asia about 6,000 years ago. Until the horse collar was invented, horses were not used to pull heavy loads, but for pulling warriors in chariots. In the Middle Ages horses were bred to be strong enough to carry knights in full armor. These thoroughbreds are among the 150 breeds known today.

Zebras (left) are closely related to horses and donkeys. They live in sociable groups, grazing on the African plains.

Frozen waters

"The decks broke up, the great beams snapping with a noise like gunfire." *Ernest Shackleton, Antarctica, 1914*

The freezing waters around Antarctica can be treacherous. In summer, the seas are dotted with large chunks of floating ice (*right*) and, in winter, the water's surface freezes into one continuous sheet of ice.

Here, one of the most incredible real-life adventures took place. In 1914, Irish explorer Ernest Shackleton was sailing through the Weddell Sea, a large gulf that cuts into mainland Antarctica. Without warning, huge sheets of ice crushed his ship, smashing its beams like matchsticks. The 28-strong crew were forced to abandon ship and set up camp on the drifting ice, but gale-force winds soon ripped their tents to shreds. Surviving on penguin meat and seaweed, food supplies soon became scarce and Shackleton was forced to lead his crew on an extraordinary trek over frozen seas to Elephant Island, a tiny land mass about 620 miles (1,000 km) below South America. Leaving some men there, he continued with five others to South Georgia Island where, after a journey of almost 1,800 miles (2,880 km), he finally reached a whaling station. The station's commander who had seen them off two years before, now no longer recognized them as they looked so wild. All 28 crew were rescued.

The sinking of the *Titanic* prompted the setting up of a special Ice Patrol to warn ships of potentially dangerous icebergs.

WHAT'S IN A NAME?

Greenland is not green (except for its coastal areas in summer), and about 85 percent of its "land" is covered by ice (above). The country was named by Viking explorers who wished to attract settlers. Natives sail in narrow canoelike boats that are the ideal shape for working their way through broken-up ice.

ARCTIC ACCIDENT-ZONES
Icebergs are dangerous because they are solid and most of their immense size is hidden beneath the water (below). Besides icebergs, the other main danger for ships in arctic waters is floating pack ice. If a ship gets stuck working its way through the huge broken sheets (left), it can be crushed to pieces as the ice pushes against it.

This boat sails between floating ice in Arctic waters (*above*). If a boat gets stuck, rescue boats called icebreakers may have to cut it free.

— Alvin

THE WRECK OF THE *TITANIC*
In 1986, the murky depths of the north Atlantic Ocean were spot-lighted by bright beams from the small, three-person submersible, Alvin (left). As the mud clouds cleared, a dark shape appeared. It was the bow of the Titanic. In 1912, this ocean liner had sunk in just three hours when it hit an iceberg on its first voyage across the Atlantic. Of the 2,220 people on board, more than 1,500 died. Many of these drowned in the icy, black waters as there were only enough lifeboats for half of the passengers.

BUTTERFLIES AND MOTHS

Butterflies and moths are called Lepidoptera, which means scale-wings. Their wings are covered with tiny scales, arranged like roof-tiles. Some scales have beautiful colors, and others bend light, like crystals, to give a rainbow sheen. Butterflies are generally more colorful than moths. They fly in the daytime, and hold their wings together upright when resting. Their antennae are club-shaped. Moths are active at night. They hold their dull-colored wings flat over their backs when resting. Some male moths have feathery antennae. Butterflies and moths undergo complete metamorphosis.

Butterfly mimics
The colorful markings on some butterflies' wings are warning colors, to deter predators. Poisonous insects advertise their distastefulness in this way. Birds soon learn to recognize these species and avoid them. Different species of poisonous moths or butterflies from the same region reinforce the message, by having very similar patterns and wing shapes. In Peru, two poisonous species, of heliconius and podotricha butterflies, look alike. This is called Mullerian mimicry (imitation). Some other butterflies which are not poisonous 'cheat' by mimicking the warning patterns of poisonous species. In North America, a species of harmless viceroy butterfly looks very like the poisonous monarch butterfly. This is called Batesian mimicry.

Podotricha telesiphe

Heliconius telesiphe

Owl butterfly
(*Caligo oileus*)

Siderone galanthis

Viceroy

Monarch

Butterflies and moths, like all insects, are cold-blooded. Their body temperature is about as warm or cold as their surroundings, since they cannot generate their own body heat, as warm-blooded mammals and birds can. Butterflies spread their wings in the sunshine to warm up and hide in the shade when they are too hot. Moths have furry bodies to retain the heat they absorb during the day, so that they can fly at night.

Disgusting disguises

The young of many moths and butterflies camouflage or disguise themselves as inedible objects, to avoid being eaten by predators. Geometer moth caterpillars look like twigs, and position themselves on branches so as to complete their disguise. The European black hairstreak chrysalis and the hawkmoth caterpillar from Central America (right) pretend to be unpleasant bird droppings.

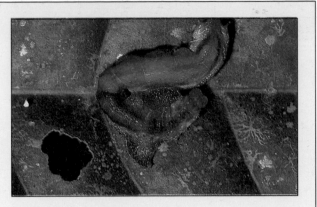

Large elephant hawkmoth

Morpho butterfly (*Morpho menelaus*)

Dasyopthalma rusina

Adapting to industry

The peppered moth is an example of how, over many generations, some species of insects are able to adapt their camouflage to fit in with a changing environment. The normal form of the peppered moth is creamy with dark speckles, difficult to see on the bark of trees. But following the Industrial Revolution in the 19th century, a new form of dark moth became common, which could hide on sooty bark.

Insect painter

Jean Henri Fabré (1823-1915) lived in Provence in France. He was a village school teacher before he turned to entomology, the study of insects. But he did not collect dead insects, like many naturalists of the time. He studied their habits by watching them in the wild.

Fabré wrote many books on insect behavior, describing each detail of their lives. He also left behind many beautiful watercolor paintings of the species he had studied.

Madame Butterfly

The opera *Madame Butterfly* was written by an Italian composer, Giacomo Puccini, in 1904. It tells of a tragic love affair between an American naval officer, Pinkerton, and a Japanese girl, Butterfly. They marry, but Pinkerton leaves, and returns years later with a new wife. Puccini's beautiful melodies convey the drama, passion and tragedy of the story.

LIZARDS

The lizard group is by far the biggest group of reptiles living today, and the most widespread around the world. In many regions, especially the tropics, lizards are a familiar sight. They hunt mainly by day, in the open, so people see them more often than other reptiles. Lizards do not have poisonous bites, except for two North American species, the gila monster and the Mexican beaded lizard. Some species, such as the Australian frilled lizard, have evolved elaborate crests or frills, to make themselves look fiercer to enemies, or to impress their mates.

Shape and form

Most lizards have a large head with prominent eyes, a slim body, four legs of equal length, and a long tail. However, this basic body shape has become adapted in many different ways, to suit various lifestyles. Some lizards that burrow rapidly in soft soil have lost their limbs, and look more like snakes. Some lizards have strong, agile limbs and grasping fingers, for moving through branches.

Flap-necked chameleon

The Komodo dragon from Southeast Asia is the largest lizard.

The Australian frilled lizard can erect a ruff of skin.

Impressing a mate

The anole lizard from South and Central America is one of many species in which the male is larger and more brightly colored than the female. He can display a flap of skin on his throat, known as the dewlap, by moving his throat bone forward to hold the flap out like a fan. The dewlap is vivid red or yellow, and its flash of color tells the female that he is courting her and wishes to mate. Flying lizards have a similar dewlap.

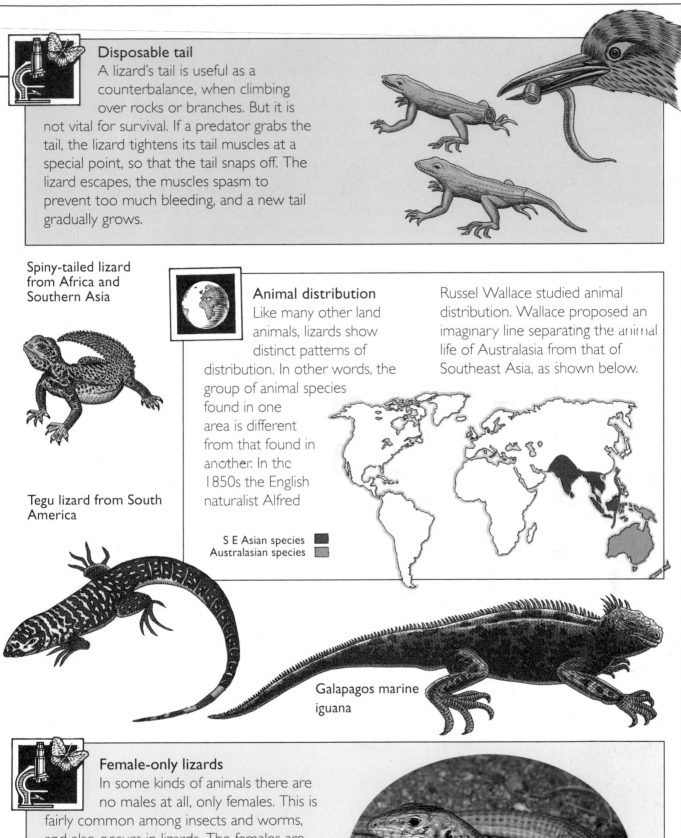

Disposable tail

A lizard's tail is useful as a counterbalance, when climbing over rocks or branches. But it is not vital for survival. If a predator grabs the tail, the lizard tightens its tail muscles at a special point, so that the tail snaps off. The lizard escapes, the muscles spasm to prevent too much bleeding, and a new tail gradually grows.

Spiny-tailed lizard from Africa and Southern Asia

Tegu lizard from South America

Animal distribution

Like many other land animals, lizards show distinct patterns of distribution. In other words, the group of animal species found in one area is different from that found in another. In the 1850s the English naturalist Alfred Russel Wallace studied animal distribution. Wallace proposed an imaginary line separating the animal life of Australasia from that of Southeast Asia, as shown below.

S E Asian species
Australasian species

Galapagos marine iguana

Female-only lizards

In some kinds of animals there are no males at all, only females. This is fairly common among insects and worms, and also occurs in lizards. The females are able to lay eggs which hatch into young without first mating with a male. This method of reproduction is called parthenogenesis. The New Mexico whiptail lizard is parthenogenetic. It has been bred in captivity for many generations, with no males at all.

RODENTS AND RABBITS

Within the order Rodentia there are 3 main groups: Squirrel group, with kangaroo rats, marmots and beavers (377 species). Porcupine group, with African mole-rats and, from South America, guinea pigs, chinchillas (188). Mouse group, with rats, hamsters and jerboas (over 1,137). The order Lagomorpha includes rabbits, hares and pikas (58 species).

Rodents, a group that includes mice and rats are extremely successful mammals, found in nearly all habitats except the sea. Most live on the ground, although there are many – such as squirrels – that are good at climbing or living in trees. Others, like beavers and some voles, live in and around fresh water. Many use burrows for shelters and homes, but mole-rats and other species are adapted to a life burrowing underground and almost never come to the surface. The secrets of their success include their feeding methods and their ability to reproduce fast. Hares, rabbits, and the similar pikas share some of the same adaptations but are not so varied.

Teeth and jaws

Rodents have a pair of large incisor teeth at the top and bottom of the front of the mouth. These grow continuously, and are used for gnawing into tough plant food, a process that wears the teeth down as fast as they grow. The enamel on the front of the incisors is hardest, so the teeth wear into a chisel shape. Along the side of the jaws are flattened chewing teeth. Rabbits have two pairs of chisel-shaped incisor teeth. They make good use of food by passing it through the gut twice, eating the feces produced the first time.

A porcupine shows its long front incisors.

Breeding

Many rodents produce great numbers of offspring. This is not so much because their litters are large – while some species produce as many as 17 young at a time, a more typical number is 4 – but because the young themselves become able to breed at an early age. In species such as mice, pregnancy lasts just a few weeks and those less than a year old may start to produce litters. In favorable conditions populations build up fast. Rabbits, too, breed fast. With no deaths, the offspring of a single pair could reach 33 million in 3 years.

House mice produce litters several times a year.

Homes

Rodents make their homes in a variety of places. Many climbing species rest in tree holes. Others make a ball nest from sticks, as do some squirrels, or from grasses or bark, as do harvest mice and dormice. Most rodent homes are not elaborate, but wood rats and stick-nest rats build large mounds of twigs to serve as weatherproof houses. These may have several compartments, including a place to store food and a latrine. The most elaborate aboveground structures are made by beavers, which make dams of sticks and mud to control water levels around the 'lodge' containing the family. Many rodents seek refuge down burrows. Some construct complex systems of tunnels with escape holes, nest chambers, storage places and latrines. Prairie dogs build a raised lip of soil around the entrance to keep out floodwater. The longest tunnels are those of mole-rats — more than 400m (440yd) long. The homes of rabbits are similar but less varied.

A beaver's dam and lodge in Alaska

Squirrels sometimes nest in holes in trees.

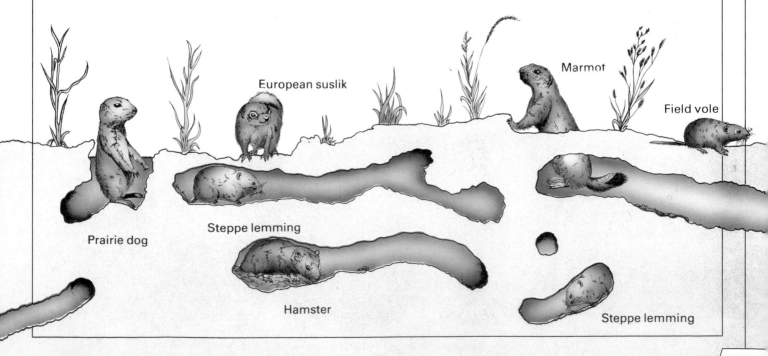

European suslik

Marmot

Field vole

Prairie dog

Steppe lemming

Hamster

Steppe lemming

KILLER WHALES?

Under the supervision of Herbert Ponting, the husky dogs were tethered on a large slab of floating ice. Suddenly the ice shuddered. Ponting looked around to see what was happening. Eight orcas had gathered beside them. Some had swum beneath the ice and were bumping it from below.

Ponting was terrified. He believed he knew exactly what was going on: The orcas were trying to get at the dogs by tipping them into the sea. Thanks to reports such as this, the orca got its undeserved reputation as the "killer whale."

PLAYFUL PIEBALDS
The beautiful black-and-white orca – also unfairly known as the killer whale – is a large, highly intelligent member of the dolphin family.

Playful, gentle, and inquisitive, they are famous for poking their noses out of the water to see what's going on. Perhaps this is what happened when the killer whales bumped the ice near Ponting. His tale even led to a U.S. Navy manual stating that orcas would "attack at every single opportunity" – completely untrue!

Beachcombers
For the orcas of the Patagonian coast of Argentina, seal pup is a great delicacy. They launch themselves right up onto the beach to grab a tender morsel (left), ignoring older seals and even a nosey camera crew in the water. There is no evidence of a so-called "killer" ever attacking a boat or a human being.

A Modern Myth
When Herbert Ponting, photographer on the British 1911 Antarctic Expedition, mistook orca inquisitiveness for aggression (main picture), he helped create the myth of the creature's murderous nature.

FREE WILLY? In the 1960s, scientists began to challenge the idea that orcas were man-eaters. When the beast's friendly nature was realized, some were put on display in ocean theme parks and taught tricks.

Further research showed that this unnatural behavior caused the creatures great stress. Though films like *Free Willy*, (1995, *left*) argued for their freedom, many orcas remain in captivity.

Narwhal

Unicorn

HORNY TUSK. The narwhal of the icy Arctic has long been regarded as an exotic creature. In the 10th century, the Vikings sold the narwhal's spiral tusk (actually a single tooth 9 feet long) to European merchants, pretending that it was a unicorn horn. England's Virgin Queen, Elizabeth I (1558–1603), kept a narwhal's tooth under her bed as she believed it had magic powers.

WHALE "SINGING"
Using modern acoustic technology, marine biologists have learned that several species of whales communicate with each other by means of low-frequency sounds ("singing") that carry many miles through the ocean.

Although we do not yet know what the different noises mean, they are further evidence of the creatures' sophisticated intelligence.

A Hard Tusk
The large tusks of the male walrus serve many functions – fighting other males, breaking holes in the ice, and as an ice pick to heave itself out of the water.

WHAT IS A HURRICANE?

A hurricane is a large, spinning wind system that develops over warm seas near the equator. These areas are known as the tropics. Technically, hurricanes are called tropical revolving storms, but they also have local names. They are called hurricanes when they occur over the Atlantic Ocean, typhoons in the Far East, and cyclones in the Indian Ocean. By definition, all are characterized by rotating winds that exceed speeds of 75 mph on the Beaufort wind scale.

The tropics are the hottest parts of the world, and experience the most extreme weather conditions. Air heated by the sun rises swiftly, which creates areas of very low pressure. As the warm air rises, it becomes loaded with moisture that condenses into massive thunderclouds. Cool air rushes in to fill the void that is left, but because of the constant turning of the earth on its axis, the air is bent inward and then spirals upward with great force. The swirling winds rotate faster and faster, forming a huge circle that can be up to 1,200 miles across.

▲ The typhoon that hit Manila in the Philippines in 1988 caused severe flooding. People were forced to cling to items like tires to survive.

▶ The shattered remains of Darwin in Australia after Cyclone Tracy hit the area on Christmas Day in 1974. Tracy's winds reached 150 mph and battered the city for over four hours. 48,000 inhabitants were evacuated and 8,000 homes destroyed.

Extreme conditions

A spectacular part of tropical storms is the long, low thunderclouds that can be seen rolling across this landscape. The tinges of gray-black at the edges of the clouds are the result of undercurrents of cold air that force the moisture in the warmer air above to condense very quickly. It is these clouds that bring the torrential downpours of rain that accompany most thunderstorms. Thunder and lightning can also occur.

WHAT IF A LEOPARD COULD CHANGE ITS SPOTS?

A leopard's spots are designed to break up its outline and keep it hidden, especially when it's crawling through the long grass, or lying on a tree branch. Many mammals have this type of camouflage – both the hunted and the hunters, including tigers. If these animals were brightly colored, or if they had strange patterns on their fur, they would stand out, and enemies could spot them at once!

Dappled deer

Adult red deer tend to graze in open areas. But baby red deer, called fawns, hide by lying still among ferns or heather, under a bush, or in a thicket. The sunlight shining through the leaves creates light and shadow below. So the fawn's coat has similar light and dark patches to conceal it in the dappled sunlight.

What if a polar bear had no fur coat?

Its naked, pinkish body would show up clearly against the white background of snow and ice. So the polar bear would have trouble trying to sneak up on seals to eat, and it would get very hungry. It would also be extremely cold. This is another job of a mammal's hairy coat – to protect against the cold (or heat, as in the case of a camel). The polar bear's fur coat is extremely thick and warm, as well as extra white. Without it, the bear would quickly freeze to death.

Stop blubbering!

All mammals have a layer of a soft, fatty substance just under the skin, covering the muscles and other inner parts. When this is very thick, it's called *blubber*. It makes the seal's body smooth and sleek, and acts as a store of energy should food ever get scarce.

However, its major role is as a wraparound blanket of fat to help the fur keep out the cold, especially when the animal is swimming in the icy seawater. Some seals can have a layer of blubber that is more than 4 in (10 cm) thick.

Fur —
Skin —
Blubber —
Muscle —

Skinny seal
A blubberless seal would not only look very thin, it would very quickly freeze to death in the cold seas that it swims through.

What if mammals had spears and armor?

Some do – the porcupine has spines and the armadillo has armor-plating. The porcupine has normal mammal fur and also very thick, sharp-tipped, spearlike hairs growing from the skin. These are quills which are only attached loosely to the skin. The porcupine can flick its tail and throw off the quills into an unwary attacker's face.

The armadillo has a covering of small bone plates embedded in horny skin, with patches of tough skin and hairs between them. The plates hang down over the creature's head, sides, legs, and tail. When threatened, the armadillo can roll up into an armor-plated ball.

159

CATS

The cat family, the Felidae, are all very similar in shape though they come in different sizes. They are all agile hunters that stalk and pounce on their prey. They have excellent stereoscopic vision, they can see in color and in the dark. They have a special layer at the back of the eye, called the tapetum, which reflects light back to the retina, so they can see in low light. All cats have sensitive whiskers for nighttime hunting.

Small Cats

There are 28 species of "small cats." Apart from their size they are very similar to big cats. Small cats can purr, but they cannot roar. Big cats can roar, but cannot purr. The domestic cat (bottom), is descended from the wild cat, which was found in Europe and North Africa. The bobcat, and the lynx (top), are peculiar in having ear tufts and short tails. Many small cats, like the ocelot, have spotted coats for camouflage in the forest.

Cheshire Cat

The grinning Cheshire cat, in *Alice's Adventures in Wonderland*, by Lewis Carroll, caused some difficulty when the Queen of Hearts ordered "Off with its head." The Cheshire cat was able to make its body invisible. The executioner was puzzled as to how he could cut a head off a body that was not there. While the king debated the matter the queen threatened to have all the court executed. Meanwhile the cat had disappeared!

Witch's Cats

Cats have lived alongside people for some 5,000 years, ridding homes of mice and rats. But in the Middle Ages they became associated with witchcraft and the devil. They were cruelly persecuted along with their owners. The Christian Church also tried to rid the world of them because they were symbols of paganism.

Record Breakers

The cheetah is the fastest land animal in the world. It can reach speeds of 60 miles per hour. It can move so fast because it stores energy in its springlike backbone. When it runs its backbone alternately stretches and coils, swinging its long legs forward and backward.

Big Cats

Tigers, cheetahs, leopards, and jaguars are solitary hunters. They usually stalk medium-sized grazers no bigger than themselves. Lions take larger prey, and hunt in prides. Prides consist of a full-grown male and several breeding females and their cubs. Big cats hunt only when they are hungry, gorging on the kill and then dozing for several days.

Tiger   Jaguar

Lion

Agility

Cats are supposed to have "nine lives" – they almost always land on their feet. They do this by a reflex action controlled by the organ of balance in the inner ear. It tells the brain which way up the cat is. The brain matches this information with messages from the eyes. The neck muscles turn the head to the upright position and the body follows – all before the cat hits the ground. Cats are agile climbers, clinging on with their claws. They have powerful legs and can spring straight up into the air, landing on their prey on all fours.

REPTILE CAMOUFLAGE

Throughout the animal world, creatures use body colors and patterns to blend in with their surroundings and merge with the background. This is called camouflage. It helps animals to hide if they are prey, being hunted by sight. It also helps them to creep up unseen on a victim, if they are hunters. The bodies of many reptiles are dull brown or green in color, to match the soils and vegetation where they live. A few are very brightly colored, to warn other animals that they are dangerous, or to advertise for mates at breeding time.

Shape
Shape is important in camouflage. The vine snake has a slim body. It resembles a vine or creeper on a tree.

Pattern
The spade-tailed gecko has a mottled pattern that blends in well with the patchy bark of trees.

Unseen in the shadows
Rudyard Kipling's exciting story *The Jungle Book* (1894) tells of how a boy, the "man-cub" Mowgli, is reared by a family of wolves in the jungles of India. One of the main characters is Kaa, a cunning and untrustworthy python. A troop of wild monkeys capture Mowgli. But Kaa arrives to help rescue him, and the monkeys are terrified. They know the stories of the great python who "could slip along the branches as quietly as the moss grows – and who could make himself look so like a dead branch or a rotten stump that the wisest were deceived, till the branch caught them." Such camouflage is even more effective at twilight and during the night, when many snakes go hunting.

Startle colors
The bright colors of many reptiles warn predators that they are venomous or that their flesh tastes horrible. This is called warning coloration. Bright colors are also used to startle an enemy. The blue-tongued skink (right) is a lizard. When threatened, it opens its mouth wide to reveal a bright blue tongue. The frilled lizard (top left) also flashes startle colors.

Changing color

Chameleons can change color to match their surroundings. Their skin color is due to tiny grains of colored pigments in cells called melanophores. The chameleon's eyes detect the color of its surroundings and send nerve signals via the brain to the skin. The signals make the melanophores shift their pigment grains, so that they are clumped together or spread out, either in the upper skin or lower down.

Pigment grains clumped

Nerves

Melanophore cells

Pigment grains spread out

Light strikes the grains and makes the skin appear a different color.

Disruptive coloration
Patches of dark color on a light body help to break up the outline of an animal, so that its overall shape is less recognizable. The Gaboon viper's coiled body is difficult to see among the fallen leaves.

Boulder ballast
A crocodile hunting its next meal lies low in the water, camouflaged as an old floating log. It drifts or swims slowly up to an unsuspecting prey animal, before seizing it in powerful jaws. The crocodile's nostrils and eyes are on the top of its head, so the reptile can see and breathe while almost submerged. Some crocodiles deliberately swallow small rocks and boulders. The extra weight of the stones in the stomach helps them to float lower in the water, and be even less noticeable.

SHARK

A SHARK IS A VERTEBRATE, but it doesn't have a backbone, or any bones at all. It has a skeleton, of course, like any other fish. But this is made of cartilage, or gristle. The flattened fish called rays also have a cartilage skeleton. Together, sharks and rays make up the cartilaginous fish group.

STURDY CARTILAGE
Compared to bone, cartilage is slightly squishy and flexible, yet still durable. It is also very light, helping to save body weight.

JAWS
Sharks have sharp teeth in their mouths – obviously. But their skin is also covered with tiny, teethlike points, called denticles.

GILL SLITS
Like other fish, a shark takes water into its mouth and passes it over the gills, which absorb dissolved oxygen.

LIGHT LIVER
Sharks lack a swim bladder. This problem is partly helped by the lightweight skeleton, and also by a huge liver. This contains lots of lighter-than-water oil, to give buoyancy.

SCREW GUTS
A shark's guts are relatively short and straight. But they have a large surface area for absorbing digested food, due to the screw-shaped spiral valve inside.

ANATOMY *AT WORK*
TOTAL TOOTH REPLACEMENT
Sharks never need a dentist. They always have new teeth. These begin on the inner sides of the jaws, and gradually grow and move forward, to the front edges. As the shark bites and feeds, they break or snap off. But more continually grow. And more...

IT WASN'T ME, HONEST!
There are about 370 different kinds of sharks. Only 20 or so attack humans regularly. They include the great white, tiger, mako, and hammerhead. Some sharklike bites may be caused by fish such as barracudas.

SALMON

THE "FLESH" OF A FISH LIKE THE SALMON is really muscle. It's the large blocks of muscle along either side of the body, which are attached to the vertebrae of the backbone. These pull alternately to bend the body from side to side, making the tail swish, which pushes the fish along.

GILL COVER
This bony plate, the operculum, protects the delicate, blood-filled gills underneath. Water that has passed over the gills exits through the slit at the rear.

BRAIN

DORSAL FIN

FIN CONTROL 1
The dorsal fin, on the back, and the anal fin, on the underside, help to stop the fish from spiraling around like a corkscrew.

SPINES ON VERTIBRAE

CAUDAL FIN

HEART AND LIVER

PECTORAL FIN (*not shown*)

STOMACH

PELVIC FIN

ANAL FIN

SCENTS AND SMELL
Each nostril leads into a chamber lined with microsensors that detect chemicals in the water. Fish like salmon have an incredibly sharp sense of smell.

FIN CONTROL 2
The paired pectoral fins on the front sides and pelvic fins on the rear sides help with steering and stopping.

MASSIVE MUSCLES
More than half the salmon's weight may be muscle. It's arranged in zig-zag blocks called myotomes, which join onto the spikes and projections of the vertebral bones.

FIN CONTROL 3
The two-lobed caudal fin at the rear provides the pushing power for swimming. Oh, and it's also called the tail.

LIFE CYCLE OF A SALMON
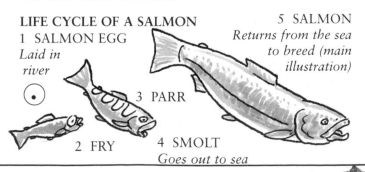
1 SALMON EGG
Laid in river

3 PARR

2 FRY

4 SMOLT
Goes out to sea

5 SALMON
Returns from the sea to breed (main illustration)

ANATOMY AT WORK
LIKE FISH OUT OF WATER
If a normal seawater fish swam from salty water into the fresh water of a river, it would take in the fresh water, swell up, and burst!

If a normal freshwater fish swam from the fresh water of a river into the sea, it would lose most of its body fluids, shrivel up, and die!

WHAT IF AN ELEPHANT HAD NO TRUNK?

The long trunk is one of the main features of the animal, and it couldn't survive without it. The trunk is the nose and upper lip, that have joined together and grown very long. The elephant uses its trunk for many vital actions, especially eating and drinking. Without a trunk, this plant-eater would not be able to pick up grass and leaves to eat. It also uses the trunk to smell, breathe, feel, and to suck up water. If the elephant crosses a deep river, it can even use its trunk as a snorkel!

Trunk call
The hairy tip of the trunk is very sensitive to touch. The two holes are nostrils that lead to the long nose tube. Through this the elephant breathes and trumpets its calls. Muscles bend the trunk in any direction.

Sniffing and smelling
Elephants lift their trunks high to sniff the air for predators, fire, and other dangers, and to catch the scent of their herd and other creatures. They also smell food before eating it.

The daily grind

Long, thin, sharp, fang-shaped teeth are good for catching, killing, and ripping up meaty prey – but they are no good for chewing or grinding up leaves, grass, fruits, and other plant parts. Herbivores (plant-eaters) need wide, broad, fairly flat teeth to mash and pulp their food thoroughly. This is because plants are made from tough fibers that need to be broken down, so that a herbivore's intestines can extract the nutrients.

Feeding

The elephant has a short neck, so its head cannot reach down to the ground or up to the trees. But the trunk can. It curls around juicy grasses and leaves, rips them off, and stuffs them into its mouth.

Communicating

Elephants touch and stroke their fellow herd members, to greet them and keep up their friendships. They also trumpet and make noises with the help of their trunk. These forms of communication are very important to the herd.

Chewing the cud

Some mammals are able to swallow their food quickly, and then bring it up again to chew over slowly. They are called *ruminants*. They include cows, antelope, and llamas.

When the food is first swallowed it goes into the rumen, the first part of the four-chambered stomach (below). The animal can then bring up this half-digested food, called *cud*, to chew over more leisurely. The cud is then swallowed into the reticulum, and then into the intestines.

Drinking and bathing

The trunk's long nasal tubes allow the elephant to suck up enormous amounts of water. This can then be flung over its back when it wishes to cool off at a watering hole. Alternatively, the elephant may be thirsty, and then it will empty its trunk into its mouth to take a drink.

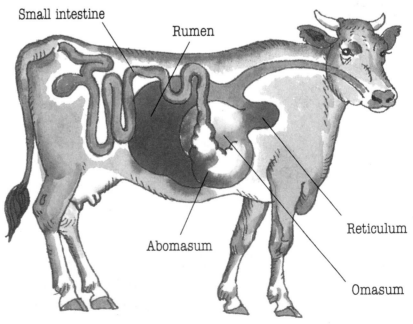

Small intestine

Rumen

Abomasum

Reticulum

Omasum

WHERE DO TREES GROW?

Trees grow all over the world, even in the harshest of conditions. They live in deserts, on mountains, in jungles, and in the icy cold. Since trees can make their own food, they are not restricted to places where food can be found, as animals are. They do, however, need sunlight and water wherever they live. Many species have developed special features which help them to survive in a particular habitat.

Desert and scrubland
Desert trees face the problem of getting enough water to live on. Baobab trees store water in their swollen trunks for use in times of drought. As they use up the water their trunks shrink.

Northern pine forest
A huge band of pine forest stretches across the top of North America, Siberia, and Scandanavia. Conifers form crowded and shady forests. They can survive even where sunlight is weak.

Mountain
Some mountain trees, such as dwarf willows and dwarf conifers, grow very close to the ground. This keeps them out of the biting winds that howl down the mountainside. They may be short enough to step over – only a few inches high. These trees are given the nickname *krummholz*, or "elfin wood."

Mangrove swamps
Bands of mangrove trees grow in tropical estuaries, where rivers meet the sea. They have to cope with large amounts of salt which would normally kill most trees. Mangrove roots have special adaptations that filter the salt out of the water they take in.

Tropical rain forests

Rain forest trees grow in dense groups. They have to compete for sunlight, and grow up to 165 feet tall to catch the sun. Rain forest trees absorb all the nutrients from the soil. When they are felled, the soil is left with so few nutrients that it is difficult for other vegetation to grow back.

The dying forests

Acid rain is killing trees worldwide. It is caused by pollution from burning gasoline in cars and coal or oil in power plants. When acid rain falls on trees it damages their leaves and releases toxic substances in the soil. Test the acid level of rain by collecting it in a clean pail. Get a strip of pH paper from your science teacher and leave it in the water for 15 minutes. Compare the strip with a pH chart to find the acid level of your sample.

Leaf damaged by acid rain

Lemon – very acidic

THE pH SCALE

Carrot

Milk

Normal rain

0 1 2 3 4 5 6 7 8 9 10 11 12 13 14

The world's biomes

The earth can be divided into regions based on the kinds of trees they support. These areas, called biomes, are largely determined by climate: temperature and rainfall are the main influences on what kinds of trees and plants grow in an area. Soil type also affects vegetation, because it is the soil that supplies nutrients for plants. The map below shows the world's major biomes.

- Tropical deciduous seasonal
- Arid grassland
- Desert
- Savanna
- Evergreen tropical
- Cool coniferous
- Mediterranean woodland
- Deciduous temperate
- Evergreen temperate

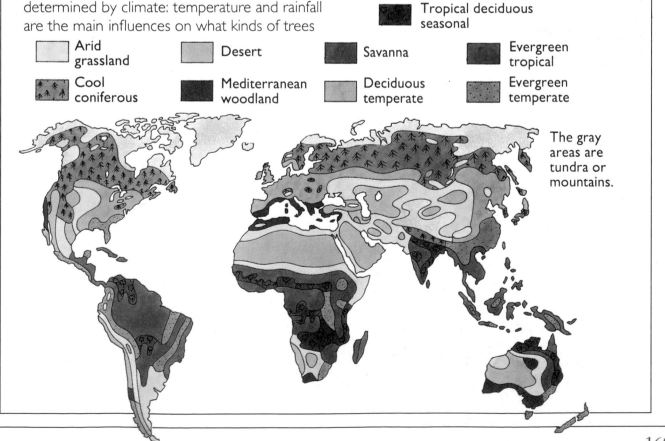

The gray areas are tundra or mountains.

WHAT ARE INSECTS?

Insects are the most successful of all animal groups, making up 85 percent of the whole animal kingdom. There are as many as 10,000 insects living on every square yard of the Earth's surface. There are many different kinds of insects, but all share a common body design, adapted to cope with every possible environment, and to eat every possible kind of food. All adult insects have a segmented body which is divided into three parts: head, thorax, and abdomen.

An insect's skin is made of a tough substance called chitin. This forms a hard shell, or exoskeleton, which protects the insect's organs. The leg and wing muscles are securely anchored to the exoskeleton. It is waterproof, and prevents the insect from drying out. But it does not allow air through. Holes in the skin, called spiracles, lead to breathing tubes. The exoskeleton does not grow. As an insect gets bigger, it must shed its old skin, and grow a new one. The outer skin, or cuticle, is patterned and colored for camouflage or warning.

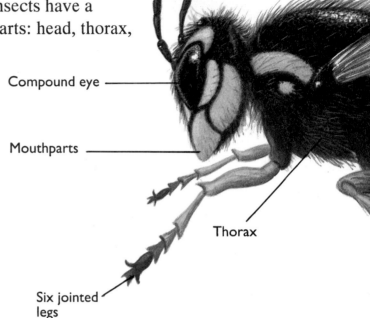

Antennae

Compound eye

Mouthparts

Thorax

Six jointed legs

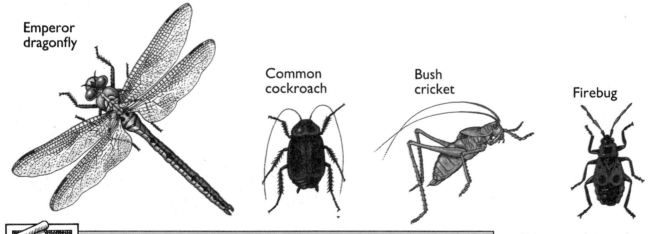

Emperor dragonfly

Common cockroach

Bush cricket

Firebug

Preserved in stone
Insects first appeared on Earth about 370 million years ago. Early species had no wings; they fed on the sap and spores of the newly-evolved land plants. Insects were the first creatures to conquer the air, 150 million years before birds first flew. This is a fossil of an early dragonfly that lived 300 million years ago, in the steamy Carboniferous forests with the ancestors of the dinosaurs.

All insects have three pairs of jointed legs, and most have four wings. Insects from some easily recognizable insect groups are shown above.

Wings

Abdomen

Spiracles carry
air inside the
body.

The head contains a simple brain which receives messages from the sense organs and controls the muscles. The thorax is made of three segments fused together. It carries the legs and wings. The abdomen contains the organs for digestion and reproduction.

Seven-spotted
ladybug
(beetle)

Bluebottle
(fly)
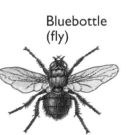

Privet
hawkmoth

Wood
ant

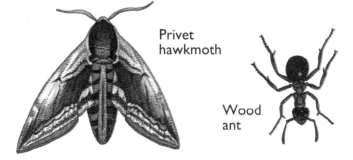

Insect relatives

Insects belong to a group of animals called arthropods. They all have segmented bodies with hard exoskeletons. But the other arthropods pictured here are not insects. Spiders have eight legs. Their body segments are fused in two parts – a head-thorax and an abdomen. Millipedes and centipedes have many body segments, with legs on each.

Millipede

House spider

DINOSAUR EXTINCTION

The most intriguing question about dinosaurs has always been "why did they die out?" There is no simple answer to this question, even though many hundreds of scientists are studying the problem. They are not studying the extinction of the dinosaurs alone, but the whole question of extinction. Many other plants and animals have died out in the past, and it is important to understand how and why this happened. Having this information could help save many species that are under threat in the modern world. Humans are causing extinctions now, because of pollution and other damage to the environment. Maybe the dinosaurs can tell us how to save the earth today, because of their extinction 65 million years ago!

Early ideas

Some of the early dinosaur scientists, 100 years ago, thought the dinosaurs died out because the air changed, and they could not breathe. Others thought that the dinosaurs disappeared simply because they became too big. They were too heavy to move without falling over, and could not find enough food to survive.

One theory is that a huge killer meteorite hit the earth. Smaller meteorites have fallen since then, making craters like this one in Arizona.

Survivors

Whatever happened 65 million years ago, most plants and animals were not wiped out. Among the reptiles, the crocodiles, turtles, tortoises, lizards, and snakes survived. So too did the mammals, birds, amphibians, fish, and most plants and sea creatures.

Tortoise

Crocodile

Perhaps huge amounts of lava poured out of volcanoes in India. This sent up vast clouds of dust that blacked out the sun, and made the earth icy cold.

Dinosaurs and people in films

A lot of dinosaur films in the past have shown people and dinosaurs living at the same time. There are often epic battles between spear-waving cavemen and dinosaurs. No human being, however, could have wrestled with a dinosaur, since the dinosaurs died out 60 million years before the first humans lived!

Evidence from fossil leaves (above) shows that climates became colder. Perhaps that was enough to kill off the dinosaurs?

Measuring rates of extinction

You've probably heard the expression "dead as a Dodo." The Dodo is just one of millions of species of plants and animals that have died out. Extinction is quite normal. However, sometimes so many species die out all at the same time that something unusual must have been going on. One of these mass extinctions happened when the dinosaurs died out.

Dodo

The final curtain

Dinosaurs were not the only animals to die out 65 million years ago. The flying pterosaurs also disappeared, as did the swimming plesiosaurs and some other reptile groups and shellfish in the sea. Many other plants and animals, however, did survive, and life on earth had returned to "normal" about 10 million years later. "Normality," of course, also meant a world without the dinosaurs. 160 million years of domination by these beasts had ended.

WHAT IS DROUGHT?

Drought is a long period with no rain or with much less rainfall than is normal for a particular area. Almost one-third of the land on Earth is prone to drought, which affects more than 600 million people.

During a drought, the soil becomes parched and cracked. The hard-baked surface cannot absorb any water, and so very little moisture is retained in the soil. The dry and dusty topsoil is worn away by wind and rain, leaving behind patches of barren land.

Drought is a natural disaster that can affect any country in the world. However, its effects are made much worse in the developing world by a number of factors. They include overpopulation, overgrazing, and cutting down trees to provide firewood.

Hot, dry winds and very high temperatures, combined with a lack of rainfall and the evaporation of moisture in the ground, produce the conditions of drought. In some areas, periods of drought alternate with periods of flood, continually destroying food crops and farmland.

Hot, dry winds

Eroded topsoil

Dried-up wells

Failed crops

◄ **Thousands of people are forced to stand in line for food after the failure of their crops through drought.**

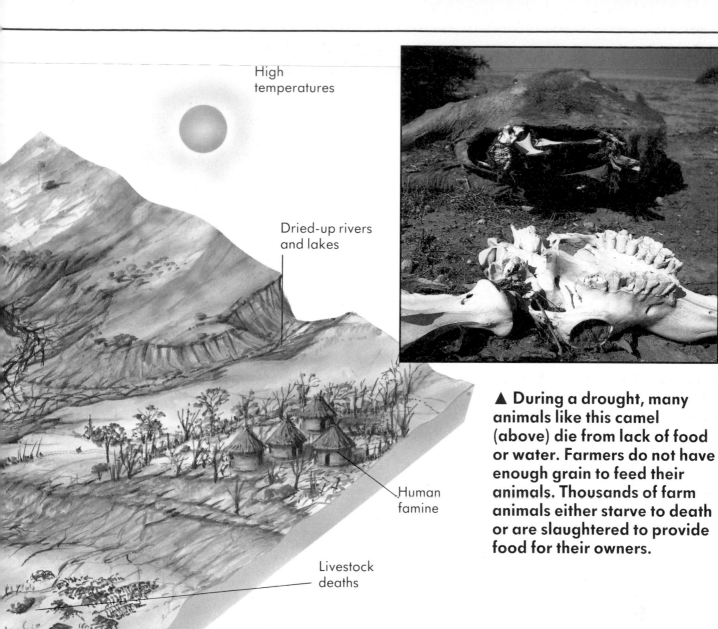

High
temperatures

Dried-up rivers
and lakes

Human
famine

Livestock
deaths

▲ **During a drought, many
animals like this camel
(above) die from lack of food
or water. Farmers do not have
enough grain to feed their
animals. Thousands of farm
animals either starve to death
or are slaughtered to provide
food for their owners.**

High temperatures

Unusually high temperatures can make
water sources evaporate very quickly.
Combined with a lack of rain, this can lead
to droughts in areas that are not normally
prone to water shortages. In 1988, temperatures in the fertile grain-growing regions
of the United States soared to record
levels. The drought that followed caused a
large reduction in the grain harvest.

BEASTS OF WAR AND MYTH

In the summer of 218 B.C. the Carthaginian general Hannibal led his army from its base camp in Spain and headed north. The Romans, thinking they were safe for that campaigning season, launched an attack across the Mediterranean on Hannibal's Spanish headquarters. It proved to be a disastrous mistake.

Hannibal took his 30,000 men, horses, and 37 elephants (see coin, *above*) across the Pyrenees and crushed the Gauls. In October, to everyone's amazement, he decided to take the Little St. Bernard Pass into Italy and launch a surprise attack on Rome itself. Fifteen days later he was in Italy, elephants and all!

Assisted by his war beasts, Hannibal won a series of brilliant victories. But in the end, deprived of support and reinforcements, he had to return home without capturing Rome.

S TEEDS OF MYTH. The importance of horses to humans is reflected by their appearance in numerous legends. The mythical centaurs were half human, half horse inhabitants of the wooded foothills. They have been popular figures in folklore since the time of the ancient Greeks.

Pegasus was a mythical winged horse born out of the blood of the monstrous snake-haired Medusa.

THE TROJAN HORSE

The world's most famous horse appears in a story from Homer's epic poem, *The Odyssey*. It was a huge model built by the Greeks for their enemies, the citizens of Troy. Odysseus and his Greek warriors hid inside the horse while the Greek army sailed away. Then the Trojans pulled the horse into the city.

Quick Victory
Once the horse was inside the walls, the Greeks opened the city gates. Troy fell soon afterward.

THE MYTHICAL UNICORN is a beautiful white horse with a single horn growing from its forehead (depicted *right* in the film *Legend*). Drinking from the horn was believed to give protection from illness.

Trunk Route (left)
The passes were blocked by snow when Hannibal led his war elephants through the Alps into Italy, fighting off local tribesmen as he went.

HANNIBAL'S HEAVIES

Once on the Italian plain, the elephants proved a useful shock tactic. But they needed to be cared for and were too slow and cumbersome to win a battle on their own.

THE SWEET SMELL OF SUCCESS!

In a story told by the Greek historian Herodotus, when Cyrus the Great of Persia's army met that of the Lydian king Croesus, the horrible smell of Cyrus' camels terrified the Lydian horses!

When their horses ran away, the Lydian cavalry were forced to jump down and fight on foot, and were soon beaten by Cyrus' troops.

Conquering Camels (right)
Camels were also used by the Arab soldiers of the 7th–8th centuries A.D. They built a vast Muslim empire stretching from Spain to Persia.

WHAT IS THE WEATHER?

From sunshine and showers to blizzards and hurricanes, the weather is a combination of wind, rain, clouds, and temperature. Believe it or not, all our weather is caused by the air around our planet warming up and cooling down. The average weather in one particular region is called the climate. In some climates, the weather stays much the same all year round. But in many parts of the world, the weather changes at certain times of year. A climate appears to stay the same, but may change quite a lot over thousands of years.

Earth moves around the Sun once a year.

Earth spins once a day.

The atmosphere
The Earth is surrounded by a thick blanket of air called the atmosphere, which is made up of five layers. Weather happens only in the layer nearest to the Earth – the troposphere. This stretches up about 7 miles above the surface of the planet, not much higher than the top of Mount Everest. The troposphere is the warmest layer of the atmosphere and contains the most moisture.

Auroras are produced when radiation from the Sun hits the outer layers of the atmosphere.

50 miles

30 miles

The Sun and Earth
The Earth moves slowly around the Sun once every year. Because the Earth is tilted, places are closer to the Sun at different times of year. This affects the amount of light and heat these places receive, and produces a pattern of changes in the weather called the seasons. The Earth also spins on its axis once every 24 hours, giving us night and day.

Weather occurs in this layer, the troposphere.

7 miles

Sun gods
Many ancient peoples worshiped the Sun as a god. They made sacrifices to the gods to keep the Sun shining. In the Aztec religion, the Sun was the warrior, Huitzilopochtli, who died every evening to be born again the next day, driving away the stars and Moon with a shaft of light.

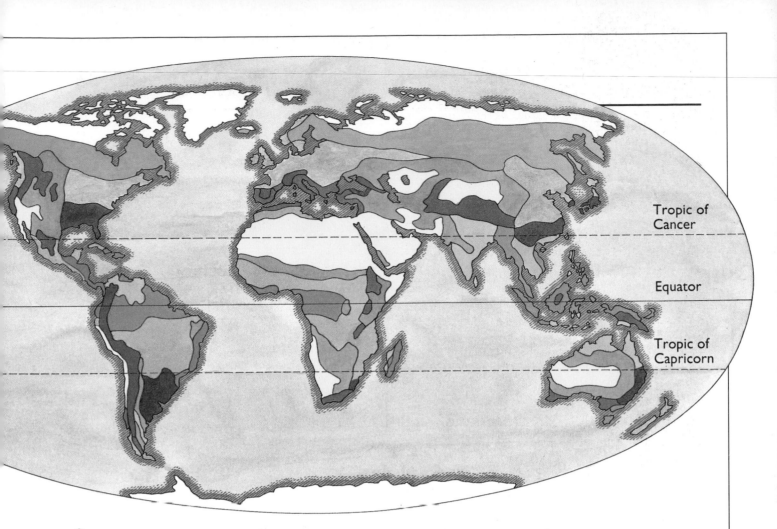

Tropic of
Cancer

Equator

Tropic of
Capricorn

Air pressure

Air pressure is caused by the force of gravity in the Earth's atmosphere pulling air down toward the surface. In 1643, Galileo's pupil, Toricelli, invented the first instrument for measuring air pressure – the mercury barometer. Before weather maps were developed in the early 1800's, the barometer was the most important tool in weather forecasting. High pressure usually indicates fine, settled weather and low pressure means cloudy, rainy weather. The French physicist, Jean de Borda (1733-1799), was the first to show that changes in air pressure were also related to wind speed. An aneroid (non-liquid) barometer measures the effect of air pressure on a chamber that has part of the air removed.

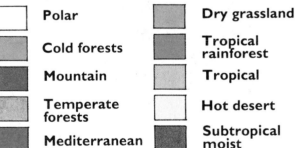

Aneroid barometer

	Polar		Dry grassland
	Cold forests		Tropical rainforest
	Mountain		Tropical
	Temperate forests		Hot desert
	Mediterranean		Subtropical moist

World climates

Climates depend on how near to the equator a place is, how high it is above sea level and how far it is from the sea. World climates can be divided into the following categories:

Polar – Cold and snowy, strong winds.
Cold forest – Short summers and long, cold winters.
Mountain – Cold and snowy high up.
  Temperate forests – Neither too hot nor too cold, rain all year round.
    Mediterranean – Long, hot, dry summers and cool, wet winters.
    Dry grasslands – Hot, dry summers and cold, snowy winters.
    Tropical rainforest – Hot, rainy, humid and wet.
  Tropical – Hot all year, wet and dry seasons.
  Hot desert – Hot and dry, hardly any rain.
Subtropical moist – Warm to hot summers, cool winters and moderate rain all year round.

WHAT IF SHEEP HAD NO WOOL?

Humans have been using animals, such as sheep, cows, and pigs, for thousands of years. These domesticated mammals have been supplying us with meat, milk, and materials. If sheep didn't have any wool, then not only would they be cold, but we would not be able to use their fleece to make our woolen clothes.

Sheep's wool is sheared, washed, cleaned, and woven into clothes, rugs, and many other woolen products.

Mammal products

Mammals produce a wide range of products that humans use directly or convert into other substances. The milk of mammals such as cows, goats, and camels is made into butter, cheese, and yogurt. We eat the muscles, or red meat. We crush and melt bones and hard pieces into glues and fertilizers. Clothes and textiles are made from the wool (mammal fur) of sheep, goats, vicunas, rabbits, rodents, and many others.

Chamois leather is the skin of the chamois, a type of goat-antelope. It is very soft, flexible, and absorbent.

A-hunting we will go

Although hunting for sport takes place in many places throughout the world, several groups of people rely on hunting mammals to survive. For example, the Inuit (Eskimo) of the far north hunt whales, walruses, and seals for their meat, bones and fur to make food, clothing, and utensils.

Bizarre pets

For as long as people have been using mammals for food, they have also been keeping them as pets. Since this time we have bred many different animals. Some of these were bred for their ability to work, such as sheepdogs, but now they are mainly for company or for show. The result has been some very strange-looking animals, such as the bulldog, whose nose is so short that it can only breathe through its mouth, the hairless sphinx cat, and the shaggy rough-haired guinea pig.

Cows provide most of our ordinary leather. They also give us a lot of meat and make most of the milk that we drink.

Pigs yield many products, from meat to pigskin for shoes. They are used to make drugs and body organs for transplants.

Arks or prisons?

Zoos have become the center of debate between many groups of people. Some people believe that keeping wild animals captive in cages is cruel.

However, zoos can play a positive role in the conservation of many species. Conservationists can breed rare creatures such as the giant panda, golden lion tamarin, and rhinoceros, to release them back into the wild and save them from extinction.

Zoos have not always been successful in saving species. Some animals, such as the quagga from Africa and the thylacine from Australia, have become extinct, despite having some specimens kept in zoos.

Golden lion tamarin

Quagga

Giant panda

Rhinoceros

Tsunamis

"The wave, like an enormous hand crumpling a long sheet of paper, crushed the houses one by one." *Eyewitness,* tsunami *in Chile, 1960*

In 1960, an earthquake in Chile started a *tsunami* that swept across the Pacific to Japan. Huge waves washed over many coastal towns, destroying 50,000 houses and killing hundreds of people.

Tsunamis are huge waves up to 100 ft (30 m) tall that are set off by underwater volcanoes (*right*) or earthquakes. Scientists use earthquake-monitoring devices called seismographs to predict when a *tsunami* will hit a particular coast.

The waves can travel at 480 miles (800 km) per hour and are devastating when they reach shallow water. They crash onto the land, washing people, animals, homes, and cars away — no sea wall is high enough to stop them. The power of *tsunamis* is so great that, in 1692, one that hit Port Royal in Jamaica threw ships onto the tops of buildings. It is said to have moved mountains and created huge splits in the earth that swallowed people whole.

WHAT ARE *TSUNAMIS*?

Tsunamis are often called tidal waves, although they are not caused by natural tides. The burst of energy from an earthquake or underwater volcano sets the sea in motion. If the waves reach shallow waters, they bunch up and become one huge — and highly destructive — wave.

The Japanese artist Katsushika Hokusai (1760-1849) made this print in 1831. It shows a huge *tsunami* tossing boats around like matchsticks.

HOLDING BACK THE WAVES

Japan suffers from many earthquakes and a large number of storms from regular typhoons. These sea defenses (right) are used to minimize the damage caused when tsunamis crash onto the shore and to help prevent flooding from storm surges. When the sea hits the defenses, the energy of the waves is reduced by the special shape of the blocks.

WAVE GOODBYE TO HOME

No, it didn't get there under its own steam — this steamer was swept into the Sumatran jungle by a huge tsunami. The tsunami occurred in 1883 after the Indonesian island of Krakatoa was blown apart by a volcano. Waves 40 ft (12 m) high destroyed coastal villages on Java and Sumatra.

Huge waves form

Waves become closer and taller near shore

When the tsunami hits land, it sweeps away everything in its path

The earthquake forces part of the seabed upward

WHAT ARE AMPHIBIANS?

Major groups: earthworm-like caecilians (150 species), newts and salamanders (350), eel-like sirens and species with minute limbs (4), frogs and toads (2,700).
Distribution: all wetlands except in polar regions.
Largest: Japanese and Chinese giant salamanders – 1.8m (6ft) long, 65kg (143lb) in weight.
Smallest: Arrow-poison frog – 8.5mm (0.3 in) long.

The name amphibian comes from two Greek words – *amphi* meaning both, and *bios* life. Young amphibians live in water. Like fish, they breathe using gills, use a tail and fins for swimming, and have a lateral line system. Adult amphibians are adapted mainly for life on land. They breathe using lungs or through their skin, have two pairs of limbs for walking or jumping, and have eyes, ears and a nose like those of true land vertebrates. Yet few adult amphibians are entirely independent of water. Most breed in water because their eggs need moisture, and amphibians dry out if their skin cannot be kept moist. Some American tree frogs, for example, spend their entire lives in trees, using rainwater "puddles" that collect at the bases of leaves to keep moist and for laying their eggs.

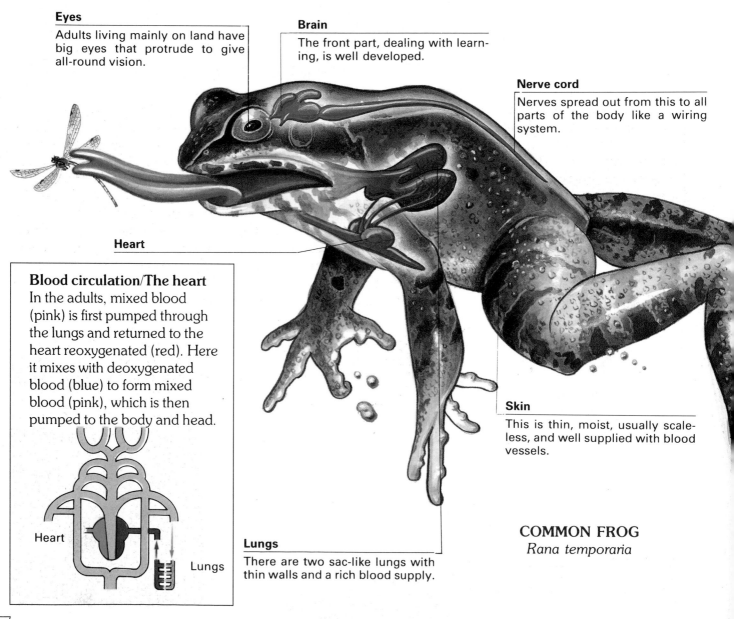

Eyes
Adults living mainly on land have big eyes that protrude to give all-round vision.

Brain
The front part, dealing with learning, is well developed.

Nerve cord
Nerves spread out from this to all parts of the body like a wiring system.

Heart

Blood circulation/The heart
In the adults, mixed blood (pink) is first pumped through the lungs and returned to the heart reoxygenated (red). Here it mixes with deoxygenated blood (blue) to form mixed blood (pink), which is then pumped to the body and head.

Heart

Lungs

Lungs
There are two sac-like lungs with thin walls and a rich blood supply.

Skin
This is thin, moist, usually scale-less, and well supplied with blood vessels.

COMMON FROG
Rana temporaria

Metamorphosis

1. Female frogs and newts lay egg masses called spawn.

2. After hatching, the larvae (tadpoles) grow gills.

3. As the legs grow, the tadpoles lose their gills.

4. Frogs lose their tail as they grow into adults.

5. Newts keep their tails and some species grow a frill along the back.

Frog

Newt

A common feature of most amphibians, and certainly of the familiar frogs and toads, is that they undergo a complete change in appearance and internal body structure during their life history. The gradual change from aquatic larva to land-living adult is known as metamorphosis. In newts and salamanders this change is less dramatic.

The adult amphibians breed in water. The female produces eggs (spawn) that are protected by a layer of jelly. After a few days to several weeks the larvae, or tadpoles, hatch. Those of frogs and toads feed on tiny water plants, whereas newt larvae eat insect larvae and small soft-shelled animals. Then, the tadpoles start to take on adult features. They begin to lose their gills, and as their lungs grow they come to the surface to breathe. They start to eat insects such as flies and worms. Legs begin to grow — first the back ones and then the front ones — and the tail gets shorter and shorter (in frogs and toads) until it disappears. The young adults are then ready to come out on land.

Skeleton

Except for lack of ribs, this is like the skeleton of true land vertebrates.

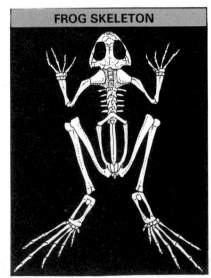

FROG SKELETON

Webbed feet

Skin between the toes of the hind feet helps to push against the water.

Monkey Business

The earliest written reports said the gorilla was a ferocious beast. It was reported to kill people and even attack elephants that disturbed it. The friendly-looking chimpanzee, on the other hand, was popular from the start. The first specimen to reach the London Zoo traveled by bus, sitting inside beside its keeper! Rarely have we been more deceived by appearances. The gorilla is a peaceful creature that lives on plants, while the chimp is one of the world's most aggressive animals. Chimps roam through the forest, leaving a trail of destruction. And it is not just the vegetation that suffers. Gangs of chimps actively hunt down monkeys and even other chimps using ruthless tactics that give their prey no chance of escape.

Monkey Spite
A baby baboon that has lost its way is viciously attacked by a troop of aggressive chimpanzees (right).

All in the Family

Humans are members of the primate family, which includes bush babies and lemurs. Apes (gibbons, chimps, gorillas, and orangutans) are our nearest relatives.

Monkeys are distant, largely tree-dwelling cousins, though baboons (*top* and *right*) spend much of their time on the ground. Several African and Asian varieties have spectacularly unattractive bottoms. Many American species have tails that can grasp objects like a hand.

APE POWER. Cartoon monkeys are usually mischievous beings, inferior to humans. This idea was turned on its head in the famous 1967 movie *Planet of the Apes*. Astronaut Charlton Heston (*above*) travels in time to find Earth run by talking apes who decide that humans like Heston are the "missing link" between them and an earlier, primitive species!

Idols or Idiots?
The ancient Chinese considered the monkey to be one of the Three Senseless Creatures. The Hindus of India, on the other hand, thought their monkey god Hanuman was clever, skillful, and loyal (right).

GENTLE GIANTS. Once called "pongos," gorillas are the giants of the ape family. The huge vegetarians, standing almost 7 feet tall and weighing 550 pounds, are famous for beating their chests. This is a sign of excitement, not anger.

Movies like *King Kong* (*below*) made many people think that gorillas were ferocious. But *Gorillas in the Mist* (1988), which told the story of Dian Fossey's study of mountain gorillas, highlighted their gentle nature.

Mystic Monkey Trio
Mythology's most famous monkeys are The Three Mystic Monkeys of Japan. *With paws covering eyes, ears, and mouth, they stand for:* "Speak no evil," "See no evil," *and* "Hear no evil" (below).

WHAT IF GIRAFFES HAD SHORT NECKS?

Some do! The okapi is a type of giraffe found in the tropical rain forests of central Africa. Unlike its taller relative, the giraffe of the African plains, all of its food is within easy reach among the lush jungle vegetation. As a result, it does not need the long neck of the plains giraffe. The tree branches of the African plains are found well above the ground, so the giraffe needs a long neck to stretch up and eat the leaves that can be over 19 ft (6 m) high. The giraffe's unique feature has evolved over years of evolution, so that it is now perfectly suited to its way of life.

Designed by committee

The odd shape of the giraffe, with its big head, long neck, long front legs, and short back legs, has often been described as an animal put together by a committee. However, the peculiar body has evolved naturally over time. The result may look odd, but it works.

Lookout post

Not only does the giraffe's tall neck allow it to reach the highest branches, it lets it see over long distances. High above the grassy plains, the giraffe can spot danger, such as a bush fire or a prowling hunter, or even new trees to eat, from several miles away.

Okapi

All creatures great and small

Just as the neck of the giraffe has developed over millions of years, so nature has created a whole host of different mammals. There are currently over 4,000 species of mammals, ranging from enormous whales to tiny mice, and from peaceful cows to aggressive tigers. Each of these has developed its own method of survival, involving a bizarre array of physical features. These include the hump of a camel, the stripes of a zebra, or the trunk of an elephant. All of these strange-looking features have evolved to help the animal survive in its environment.

The long and short of it
A giraffe, like all other mammals, including the okapi, has only seven vertebrae in its neck. However, these neck bones are greatly elongated (stretched), allowing the giraffe's head to stand way above the ground.

Giraffe

What if dinosaurs were still alive?

Then we would not be here! Mammals and dinosaurs first appeared at the same time, about 200 million years ago. However, it was the dinosaurs who were first to develop and rule the Earth. Mammals could not compete, and they had to be very small to survive. Then, mysteriously, the dinosaurs died out about 65 million years ago, and mammals were able to develop into their many and various forms (see above). If the dinosaurs were still here, then the largest mammal would probably be about the size of a cat.

INDEX

eyes 10, 99, 102, 121, 138, 161, 163, 184

fall 72, 137
families 99
famine 114
fangs 70, 122
fat 159
feathers 101, 142
fertilizers 34
fins
  caudal 65, 165
  dorsal 66, 165
fireflies 32
fish 50, 51, 64, 65, 112, 113, 129, 130, 131
flesh 165
flies 102, 171
flight muscles 10
flippers 135
flock 56
floods 20, 156
flowers 86, 138
fog 94
food 100, 135, 167
food chain 17, 35
food web 17
forests 104, 186, 188
fossils 25, 117, 142, 143
frogs 112, 130, 184
fruit 106, 107
fuels 46
fur 18, 40, 41, 98, 159, 180

Galileo 179
gavial 13
gecko 162
geologist 143
gestation period 8
gills 79, 96, 113, 165, 185
giraffes 99, 188, 189
glacier 119
glowworms 32
goats 114
goldfish 132
gorillas 99, 187
grass 119, 145
grasshoppers 114
greenhouse effect 46
guinea pigs 152
gull 129

gullet 135
gut 10

habitats 12, 123, 132, 145, 168
hailstones 118
hamsters 152, 153

Hannibal 176
hare 125
harvest mice 152
hatch 121
hawks 57
heart 10, 184
heartwood 140
hedgehog 40
herbivores 116, 166
herd 167
herons 101
hibernation 72, 137
hierarchy 18
Himalayas 59
hooves 144, 145
horses 52, 144, 145, 174
howl 90
humans 90, 91, 109, 180, 186
hummingbirds 23, 44
hurricanes 20, 156
husky 19
hyena 90
Icarus 44

ice 94, 95, 146, 154, 158, 159
ice age 46, 118, 119
icebergs 146, 147
icebreakers 147
incisors 152
Indian Ocean 156
insectivores 80
insects 10, 26, 27, 48, 49, 86, 101, 114, 122, 132, 138, 143, 148, 149, 170
intestines 166
Inuit people 12
invertebrates 52, 138

jackal 19
jaguars 63, 161
jaws 90, 143, 163

kangaroo rats 152
kangaroos 11
kiwis 45
koala bears 109

lakes 112
larvae 33, 49, 132, 185
lava 36, 37, 172
leather 181
leaves 98
legs 131, 138, 150
leopards 159, 161
light 107, 110, 148
lightning 104, 157
lions 62, 63, 74, 161
litters 152
lizards 38, 54, 67, 89, 150, 151, 172
llamas 145, 167
lobsters 52, 79, 128

locusts 114
London, Jack 91
lynx 160

magma 36, 126
mammals 8, 38, 40, 42, 56, 80, 89, 92, 98, 99, 107, 112, 120, 121, 122, 123, 144, 148, 152, 158, 172, 181, 189
mangrove trees 168
marble 127
marmots 152, 153
marsupials 8, 108, 109
marsupium 9
matriarch 99
meat 145
melon 14
metamorphosis 148, 185
meteorite 172
mice 152, 153
microscope 143
migration 25, 73, 115, 123, 145
milk 98, 181
millipede 171
mist 94
mollusks 78, 79
monkey 187
monotremes 8
monsoon 21, 73
moon 91
moths 48, 49, 148, 149
mountains 59, 127
muscles 40, 134, 151, 159, 166, 171
mussels 112

narwhal 155
nerve 163
nests 92
newts 185
nocturnal animals 81
nostrils 93
nutrients 12, 166, 169

INDEX